Make Money, Be Happy

D1464832

PEARSON
Prentice Hall
BUSINESS

Books that make you better

Books that make you better. That make you *be* better, *do* better, *feel* better. Whether you want to upgrade your personal skills or change your job, whether you want to improve your managerial style, become a more powerful communicator, or be stimulated and inspired as you work.

Prentice Hall Business is leading the field with a new breed of skills, careers and development books. Books that are a cut above the mainstream – in topic, content and delivery – with an edge and verve that will make you better, with less effort.

Books that are as sharp and smart as you are.

Prentice Hall Business.
We work harder – so you don't have to.

For more details on products, and to contact us, visit
www.pearsoned.co.uk

Make Money, Be Happy

How to make the money you want
and do the things you want to do

Carmel McConnell

Harlow, England • London • New York • Boston • San Francisco • Toronto • Sydney • Singapore • Hong Kong
Tokyo • Seoul • Taipei • New Delhi • Cape Town • Madrid • Mexico City • Amsterdam • Munich • Paris • Milan

PEARSON EDUCATION LIMITED

Edinburgh Gate
Harlow CM20 2JE
Tel: +44 (0)1279 623623
Fax: +44 (0)1279 431059

Website: www.pearsoned.co.uk

First published in Great Britain in 2005

© Pearson Education Limited 2005

The right of Carmel McConnell to be identified as author of this work has been asserted by her in accordance with the Copyright, Designs and Patents Act 1988.

ISBN: 0 273 675605

British Library Cataloguing-in-Publication Data
A catalogue record for this book can be obtained from the British Library.

Library of Congress Cataloging-in-Publication Data

McConnell, Carmel
    Make money, be happy : how to make the money you want *and* do the things you want to do /
Carmel McConnell
    p. cm.
    ISBN 0–273–67560–5
    1. Finance, Personal–Handbooks, manuals, etc. 2. Success–Handbooks, manuals, etc.
    I. Title

HG179.M37427 2005
332.024–dc22

2004043160

All rights reserved. No part of this publication may be reproduced, stored in a retrieval system, or transmitted in any form or by any means, electronic, mechanical, photocopying, recording or otherwise, without either the prior written permission of the Publishers or a licence permitting restricted copying in the United Kingdom issued by the Copyright Licensing Agency Ltd, 90 Tottenham Court Road, London W1T 4LP. This book may not be lent, resold, hired out or otherwise disposed of by way of trade in any form of binding or cover other than that in which it is published, without the prior consent of the Publishers.

10 9 8 7 6 5 4 3 2 1
09 08 07 06 05

Designed by designdeluxe
Typeset by 10pt Iowan Old Style by 70
Printed and bound by Bell & Bain Limited, Glasgow

The Publishers' policy is to use paper manufactured from sustainable forests.

This publication is designed to provide accurate and authoritative information in regard to the subject matter covered. It is sold with the understanding that neither the authors nor the publisher is engaged in rendering legal, investing, or any other professional service. If legal advice or other expert assistance is required, the service of a competent professional person should be sought.

The publisher and contributors make no representation, express or implied, with regard to the accuracy of the information contained in this book and cannot accept any responsibility or liability for any errors or omissions that it may contain.

Contents

SECTION 03

SECTION 04

Introduction

> The improvement in prosperity over the last 30 years has had no effect on reported levels of life satisfaction or happiness in the UK and that is quite remarkable. This is a serious challenge for policy makers as it appears to be very difficult to make people happy in the Western world.
>
> Andrew Oswald, Professor of Economics, Warwick University, interviewed by *The Guardian*, May 2004

Forget either/or. What about both?
Make Money, Be Happy Carmel McConnell,
to no one in particular, April 2004

01

How are you?

I hope you don't mind me asking. And one other thing. Where did you wind up putting that pencil tip?

Taking a typical week in your life right now, would you say your work generates enough happiness? And at the end of that week, do you generally make a financial profit?

I realize these are not questions you get asked every day. If someone wants to know about your career success, questions stay with topics like the role, the salary package, the remit. "How happy does your job make you?" seems beside the point, personal, intrusive even. To create a successful life, I would argue that it is essential to develop ambition and know-how about both finance and fulfilment. And to plan each one of them, rather than hope the job delivers both, equally.

If you were able to identify your place on one of the four states, great. If you would like to, I'd like to help you move your story forward, using those four states as overall reference points to consider. You could describe the journey as "toward more success" or "creating greater personal fulfilment", or "enjoying more financial reward". Those phrases are welcome, I understand, in these early stages of a personal development title. Which is fine by me, because my role is to help you *Make Money, Be Happy*.

Whatever you plan to do, the foundation work is the same. If you would like to gently, surely, properly move your story forward, first of all you'll benefit from understanding how you got to where you are now. That means exploring your beliefs, behaviours and your commitment to action. This is covered on page 120 onwards. The exercises and ideas are intended to encourage you to take some first steps towards the life you want to lead.

The goal here is to answer some of the incessant questions that emerge from this multiple choice career era.

Questions like

- What do I want to do with my life?
- Could I earn more elsewhere?
- What are my peers doing, and am I falling behind?
- Should I take time off to study, or travel?
- Could I restructure the job, go part-time perhaps, to enjoy life more?
- Is meaningful, purpose-filled work only available full-time and in certain professions?
- Can I make all the money I want, from the things I want to do?

Those questions have an almost tidal urgency, flooding in when the job becomes unbearable, or when debt hammers on the door, ebbing away when things seem OK, when something good happens at work, when there's enough money to enjoy life. The ebb and flow of big questions can lead to a feeling that life controls us, rather than us controlling life. Clearly some things are not in our gift (see King Canute, Beach Scene, 1020 AD), but just because we have little personal jurisdiction over global markets or interest rates doesn't mean we can't gain greater control in many areas. That is the goal of this book, to help you gain more control, specifically in two areas.

1 Your ability to create and keep money.
2 Ditto, happiness.

Feel in control?

Let's see. If you feel less in control than you'd like, you are not alone. Some of that perceived loss comes, in my view, from so many choices. I think we're becoming over-burdened with career questions, some caused by more flexible employment market conditions, some by new social habits. You want to design a bespoke career, well, go for it.

You can choose to:

- Get on the corporate fast-track.
- Or take a career sabbattical.
- Be a loyal brand lifer, make steady progress to the top of the tree.
- Employ others to do what you used to do, and live on the profits.
- Contract specialist skills to multiple employers for a higher rate.
- Become a so called "new authentic", cashing home equity to fund inner serenity.
- Take a gap year, or take your laptop to the beach each year.
- Retire early, consult to business once a week for a huge fee, buy the vineyard.
- Spend more time with your customers, or with your family.
- Spend more time shopping, which in turn means you have to keep working.
- Commute five minutes from bedroom to study.
- Commute five hours Barcelona – Birmingham for three office days.
- Keep work well away from home (e.g. an email-free zone).
- Turn your office desk into your home.
- Enjoy the buzz of being 24/7/365, globally mobile, wired, fired up.
- Choose to live slow, local, organic, natural, relaxed.

Whatever you choose, one thing is sure – striving for a life with more choice can be exhausting. And the stakes are high. Psychologists have shown that less perceived control at work (in terms of low autonomy and work satisfaction) can create increased risk of coronary heart disease.[1]

---

[1]Low job control and the risk of coronary heart disease in the Whitehall II study. Reported in the 1997 *British Medical Journal* 314, pages 558–65, H. Bosma *et al.*

I hope that some clarity on those big issues will give you more perspective on a myriad of other choices which may be whirling round in your head.

Some argue that a flexible, global employment market gives individual employees more choice, greater mobility and selling power. Others say it means more pressure in terms of reduced job security, downward pressure on wages and upward pressure in terms of performance. Whatever your perspective, I suggest that those able to make decisions, rather than leave them to others, are going to wind up better off. This book can help you build the kind of thinking and personal responsibility to navigate that uncertain job market. Unless you've got the whole thing sussed already.

I'm guessing that is not the case. The fact that you picked this book suggests there is room in your life for improvement, particularly in the areas of happiness and money. I really hope you are here because you want to make money and/or be happy based on who you really are. Because this book is going to show you how.

After we've sorted this out, surely a short chapter on lasting world peace and the cure for the common cold? OK. I admit this is an ambitious journey. That's why I strongly suggest you scribble notes all over the place as you go – as a way to re-engage if you are on autopilot. Or as a way to capture your ideas. You are more in control than you think, even though right now you might feel that the whole fabric of your life has been decided elsewhere.

Did you consciously decide on the life you currently occupy, or did it just happen?

Do dreams come true? How to generate other streams of income, if the choice is a not-for-profit career path.

Who can coach me? Key techniques, summarized in one formula: to *Make Money, Be Happy.*

What this book will give you

One of my big assumptions when writing this book, is that you would like to have someone on your side when you consider tough decisions. That is important. Other outcomes from reading this will, I hope, include

- a new and different perspective (let's say optimistic, better informed, pro-success) on how to manage your life;
- advice on how to make the best of your current circumstances, so that you earn more and/or feel more fulfilled;
- exercises and guidance to help you figure out where you are now, and where you want to aim for;
- a review of what is happening in terms of workplace trends. Is it really fragmenting into a myriad of personal career choices?
- ideas on how to improve the likelihood of your success, by your own definition;
- some clarity on what is really important in your life.

The chance to seriously improve your life may come as a mixed blessing. When underlying questions seem big and daunting, the do-nothing alternative becomes an easy choice. That's why so many of us are in sweet denial, rut-like routines and, oops, where did that five years go? It's not that we're unambitious, it's just easier to go with the flow. I have no sugar pills either, just some good news about the immediate benefits of taking the blinkers off about your life. You are meant to be a success story, even more of a success story than you are now. You are the best, and probably only, person to make it better.

With big questions like "how can I make more money?", we will be breaking things down into manageable chunks of suggestions, exercises and examples. Most of all, the improvements will be through small steps rather than large, unrealistic leaps.

I run regular seminars and workshops using some of these ideas, and an observation I've made is this. If there is one thing some people want more than success, it is one good enough reason why they can't have it. Something that gets them off the hook, big time. The "I could have been a contender" nearly-miss success story which gets trotted out along with the "but it wasn't meant to happen" excuse. It's like not worrying about homework if your dad gave your teacher a sick note – but for grown-ups. Do you know someone who has settled for a semi-credible reason why they can't *Make Money, Be Happy*, ending their story there and then?

The sad thing is, those who spend their life maintaining excuses get exactly the same amount of time to be alive as those who just try to make a go of it, whatever. Those in the excuses group choose to live frustrated and feel cheated and hard done by. They create elaborate coping strategies. Those who try to *Make Money, Be Happy* live stimulated, varied, self-directed lives. Which one do you want? Now is as good a time as any to make your mind up.

Work that asset

Your brain I mean. The biggest asset creator on the planet and the one you'll be working throughout this book.

Whichever of the four states you decide to go for, success depends on your capacity to think things through, to weave the pros and cons into one decision. Then act on it. This book will help you through the mists of uncertain career choices, all based on one constant anchor – the common human need for a life full of purpose and meaning.

But why get so hung up on fulfilment and purpose? Surely it is a question of choice. Some people don't want big purpose, just a reliable 9-to-5 and enough energy for afterwards. My feeling is that most of us aspire to a career that engages and stimulates. But somehow, many of us end up in debt, with few choices other than to do the nearest available work simply because it pays the bills. For many people, the idea of being fulfilled at work is just ridiculous. For many others, the idea of working at something that doesn't offer fulfilment is just as ridiculous. This is quite a split – and one that has some rather murky market-based causes.

Let me declare my bias here. I believe that every single person holds the potential for success, greatness and real personal happiness. I really do. However, economic factors cause many of us to settle for survival rather than living our true potential. Take whatever job comes up, just play it safe, hope for the best, enjoy what you can, count your blessings. This underplaying of life's potential cannot be right – surely it is a waste of huge, unique human capacity. Your capacity. You and I have been given the chance to write our own job description for the full-time role of a fulfilled, loving, prosperous person. Key performance indicator – effective at generating personal happiness and sufficient money to achieve ambitions. Do you want to pass that task onto someone who doesn't have a clue about what makes you tick? Or would you rather be the one who designs a happy life for yourself? It really is up to you.

While the stress of debt, or a hard job, can cause your hope to cloud over, there are still ways to move forward. First of all, you

Life offers two ways of thinking. "I'll wait and see how it goes" or "this is how I want it to go". Which do you prefer?

can choose to think about what makes you happy, and in your mind, design the kind of life which would allow you to be your own person, enjoying your work and becoming prosperous. There is nothing to stop you thinking in an unlimited way about your own success, even if your current circumstances are constrained in other ways. Although clever capitalism has made billionaires out of the few who create or take control of assets that make money, many of us can become more powerful, economically and in our workplace aspirations.

Personal choice in the workplace is closely linked, in my view, to personal consumer choice. The more we take control of our spending, the more workplace choices appear. Let me explain that.

The more we buy, the more we need the certainty of income, that is, the less we feel able to risk taking career choices which may not provide the necessary level of income. So what I call "the stress of stuff" (wanting it, buying it, looking after it, paying for it) in turn creates the stress of unloved work, the urgent need for a secure but potentially unfulfilling occupation. Our debts can cause us to become trapped into needing the promotion, the good opinion of some boss or organization. In a fairly seamless way, the holiday becomes a large debt plumping up your credit card balance. The need to pay the debt means this underwhelming job. Another "go away" Monday morning. So you book another holiday and the cycle of debt continues.

You and I, despite the marketing messages to the opposite, are not broken, needing to be fixed, or made over. We are not lost souls, needing to prop up sad, incomplete identities with more and better possessions. We're actually fine. Good even. Want to take your debt away? Wake up to the fundamentally fabulous person you are, here and now, reading this, today, now. You are unique, gorgeous, capable. Even without the stuff you plan to buy next. What did you say you were saving for? What if you didn't really need it? What if you were good enough, without the expensive jeans, house, car, holiday in Florida. Whatever.

Believe this and I reckon you start to take back control. Believe you are fine as you are and take a step outside the "punter to be sold more stuff to" camp, into the world of more conscious consumption. What do you really need? What really makes your heart sing? Probably not all the stuff you've got recently, though you might be doing dog hours to pay for it.

> Consumerism is a way of life that offers neither psychological or social satisfaction. A growing number of studies show that people in industrialised countries do not feel any more happy or satisfied as average income grows beyond the level to meet basic physical needs. Groups and families that had developed a culture of consumption where they only bought what they needed had cut household resources and waste. At the same time they had strengthened their sense of community involvement, personal fulfilment and quality of life.

Policies for Sustainable Consumption, OECD report, September 2003

So, one simple way to improve career choice could be to identify your real, rather than imaginary, consumer needs. That might bring more freedom to look at the kind of work you most want to do, rather than the work you have to do.

This concept of being good enough is key to your journey through *Make Money, Be Happy*. Good enough is not a message you'll hear from those nice advertisers. Imagine. "For three days

"I am fine as I am and I don't need to buy any more stuff, thank you." Possibly the most powerful personal statement possible in this over-loaded marketplace.

only, the Friendly Superstore near you will close in recognition of the fact that you've all spent millions this year on our fabulous items . . . " Er. No. That's not how it works.

And (quick point about how this situation came to be) US car maker Henry Ford made the big leap with Model T cars, priced so his workers could buy them – in any colour, as long as it was black. This was a brilliant idea, great for him, great for the workers who now had affordable transport. Instant, sustainable capitalism – heading off the crisis foreseen by Karl Marx who thought that over-production would crowd markets, causing reduced prices and therefore a crisis in capitalism. And no, he didn't see you and I working hard to buy the stuff we make at profit for our employers. Clever adaptive capitalism. Now, nothing wrong with profits – just not profits at any cost. The loss of choice about how to spend a life seems a pretty high cost to me.

So I ask you to be equally clever, to use your best asset to figure out when you are being sold the concept of being a good, pliant employee or, just as scary, a good, pliant consumer. You have your own intellectual asset which can do a brilliant job if you ask some good questions. What do I really want to do with my life? How can I make a good amount of money doing that? What do I really have to own? What am I being sold?

You have an incredible asset creator sitting between your ears. Every single success story on the planet has started with the power of individual thought – and it is 100% likely to be the same with you.

Are you niche, or commodity?

Are you niche, or commodity? Or, put another way, where are you on the economic bargaining scale? A niche product is pre-

> Economic survivors = the have nots = labour sold as commodity.
>
> Self-actualizers = the haves = labour sold as premium or niche.
>
> Which one are you?

mium, scarce, high value. A commodity is the opposite. Most of us sell our labour on the open employment market; turn up at work and get paid for being there – cash for presence. My question is, do you sell your labour as niche or commodity? My suggestion is that the employment market splits into roughly two groups. First, those who work because of the need for money, the survival deal I mentioned above. Second, those who work to self-actualize, with the emphasis on meaning and purpose from their work. Or you could say the economic have-nots and the haves, because that's roughly how it seems to work.

Now I can hear you arguing that exceptions exist. Of course they do. But how many do you know?

Labour gets sold for a wage, to pay for living costs, and like any other over-supplied commodity, it sometimes gets sold cheaply, with few frills. The employment market is simply that – a market for the sale of labour. So, without leverage in that market, the under-qualified among us take any economic survival route, which normally means low-grade, repetitive and under-stimulating work, with very little social status.

Does that mean that those of us in that situation give up on the search for meaning and purpose? Absolutely not. We just seek it outside the workplace. Us humans are natural purpose seekers – if we don't find it at work, we'll find it by being a football fan, or a doting parent, or a band-worshipping teenager. We are social mammals, with a strong need to belong and to do useful things. If we can't feel that sense of belonging and usefulness, we suffer.

So that's the story of the commodity worker. If, on the other hand, you're in demand, the market offers all sorts of lovely rewards for the worker who can sell labour as a niche product. As the proud owner of an under-supplied skill, for example, if you are a rocket-brain maths graduate ideally suited to investment bank derivatives trading, you can choose from a market rich in incentives. Your economic bargaining power allows greater choice of work, greater access to roles which are, by definition, stimulating, non-repetitive and linked to high status. Get a maths first from university and you have a number of options. Choose high financial reward – go forth young banker. Or private sector consultant. Choose high fulfilment – go forth

Niche	Commodity	Which am I right now?
For example, stuntman, celebrity chef	For example, walk-on film extra, burger flipper at local café	Niche (N) or commodity (C) labour supplier? Mark N or C below . . .
Scarce supply in the marketplace	Good supply in the marketplace	
Value and relationship driven	Cost driven	
High buyer loyalty (i.e. employer or customer)	Low buyer loyalty (i.e. employer or customer)	
Well known	Unknown	
Higher value	Lower value	
Strong competitive position	Weak competitive position	
Represents quality	Represents quantity	

young socio-political economist. Or funding expert for a high-purpose charity. Choose both – well, that's the new holy grail.

My bias comes from my experience. There is a vicious circle that goes something like this, if work choices are based simply on pay:

- Take job because of pay. Economic necessity is the driver.
- Become bored by content, disconnect from the job, stop being interested and learning.
- Under-perform.
- Remain bored, but stuck. Perhaps move sideways for a change.
- Repeat process.
- Fail to gain success, feel little real connection to work or work issues.

Versus the virtuous circle of work based on purpose.

- Take job because of interest and meaning (as well as economic need, probably).
- Become stimulated by content, learn and develop.
- Work hard because interested, engaged and energized. Do well.
- Gain promotion to even more challenging role.
- Repeat process.
- Gain ongoing career success through desire to improve in an area of interest.

The question is, which circle are you moving in right now? Please give one of the next two sentences a mental tick.

1 My work stimulates me and gives me a sense of personal challenge.

2 My work bores me and gives me a sense of personal exhaustion.

Well. That's good to know.

Now, if you move in a vicious, not virtuous circle right now, don't worry. The key here is to recognize we are all in transition, moving to somewhere better. You are not embedded in any lifestyle, even though your fear might suggest that you are. During the next few pages you'll be asked to consider what your situation, and motivation really is.

For example, if you remember the grid right back at page ix we'll consider which of the following strategies would work best for you – based on your current location.

The strategies can be summarized as follows under the next four sub headings.

Make purposeful profit

(If you found yourself in the top-right corner on the grid, or want to be there.)

Would you like to make the right amount of money, doing the thing you most want to do? Work that feels most meaningful, purposeful, fulfilling to you. This is an integrated strategy for both money and fulfilment.

Fund your fulfilment – the dual strategy

(If you found yourself in the top-left corner of the grid, or want to be there.)

When what you love to do doesn't pay the bills. This is where you will learn how to create a separate income strategy to ensure you retain the ability to do work that most fulfils you. You don't give up on your dreams because of the need to pay the mortgage.

Anywhere's better than this . . .

(If you found yourself in the bottom-left corner of the grid – does anyone actively choose to be there?)

The question is how to move from low-pay, low-fulfilment work to a better place. The bigger, happier choice is to be anywhere but here. Anywhere else becomes a big other. This is about the first steps to happiness and money.

Resign from lying

(If you found yourself in the bottom-right corner of the grid, or want to be there.)

Consider how to gently detach from a job which undermines the true you, so you can uncover what you really want. Do you want to resign from a life of compromise, and start to build opportunities based on your real priorities? This section considers how to make money, but this time without loss of your soul. This is also an excellent staging post if you've moved from the bottom-left corner of the grid.

The danger of leaving your success to others (and a quick quiz to find out if you are)

Most of us inhabit a workplace which rates individual performance against objectives, appraises and advises and aims for improvement. In the context of our working lives, it might be sensible also to consider individual economic performance. But we don't seem to. The concept of having financial objectives, and appraising ourselves against those seems overly calculated, scheming almost. Much better to muddle along and hope for the best.

Trouble is, the economic landscape has changed, with far more complexity in our personal financial decisions. We have to figure out, at an individual level, questions of pension, mortgage, debt and how to juggle quality of life with multiple spending choices. It can be overwhelming, and my suggestion is that without better understanding of the factors influencing our individual, personal economies, we are at greater risk not only of being ripped off, but also becoming economically too powerless to achieve our purpose. These are big stakes to play with.

And I feel strongly that the right amount of financial knowledge is not out of reach, it just requires the initial courage to say "I am willing to look at how I deal with money".

For those of you who had to briefly leave the page just now, perhaps ashen and a little nauseous, I do hope the following pages will return colour to your cheeks.

Let me describe this new way of thinking by drawing an analogy to business. If you were a firm, let's say one which makes furniture, you would have two main areas to manage. First, to manage the content (the making and distribution of furniture) and second, the process (the managing of money). The two would be done separately and distinctly. Your joy in life might come from being a carpenter, turning wood, but your ability to continue would be more about being a financier, turning investment into a profit. Likewise, I suggest whole life success has two parts. The content (i.e. what your work contains), as well as the process (creating enough money to fund your life). And, as we will explore, the two are not automatically connected. Do you automatically expect a carpentry shop to make a profit? No. Do you automatically expect a full-time employee to make a profit? Well, you just wouldn't think in those terms. Probably. On page 140 we will look at how to increase the likelihood that you can make a profit from what you do. And on page 211 we'll consider how to create income even if your job is never going to return a profit. That does happen and it is fine as long as you are able to create income elsewhere.

Are you willing to ask life for more happiness, as well as more money, balanced according to your values? My contention is that many of us are on autopilot, not exactly living (as Henry Thoreau said) "lives of quiet desperation" but certainly lives with debt, lacking inspiration. Something of a waste, given our unlimited human capacity for all kinds of success and pleasure. You don't need me to tell you how unique you are. Or maybe you do. It seems to be the case that the workplace is a low-compliment environment. The truth, however, is that you are capable of creating your own remarkable success story, without it feeling over-planned, canned or standard. You have created a bespoke journey so far, I imagine with a degree of success already. The question is . . .

> How can you move your story forward toward greater money and happiness – whatever the current situation?

There is more on offer. To find out how much, I need to start by asking you a few (admittedly big) questions. Just write the "yes" or "no" answer that comes to mind first.

Whatever your specialism, your overall goal is to create your own bespoke, successful life. Why are we unused to ambitious

Hugely intrusive question	Yes or no?
Does your current choice of career make you happy?	
Do you feel you make enough money?	
Does your work feel worthwhile and purposeful?	
Do you know how money has been made, by those individuals who have lots of it?	
Would you change job, if you received a great deal of money?	

> I'd like to suggest that your true career is one in success design. Creating bespoke success, tailored to your unique needs. Can you do that?

life design? In my view, it is because when you want something, you also have to carry in your heart the potential pain of not having it. If you ask, you risk rejection. And not all of us are up for that. Better to say you're not bothered anyway and do something that doesn't mean so much, and doesn't carry the same potential to hurt. At one extreme, I could talk about wasted talent, wasted years, the loss of multiple moments of happiness. In your case, I am going to take an intrusive guess and suggest that it would be nice for you to know your life is one you'd want to keep more or less unchanged, even if you happened to win the lottery. I could be wrong.

A lot of my work has been to help people renew the connection to their souls, to start believing that life can be fulfilling, prosperous. Ambitious to the point of raw sometimes. Imagine you had a very good friend who wants you to achieve your potential. Sitting opposite you now. What would their first and most obvious bit of advice be to you?

The tricky bit is getting room for some perspective – so use the imaginary best friend whenever you can. Perhaps best to not get into heated discussions with that imaginary friend in public places, just for appearances sake.

> Would you change anything about your life if a couple of million turned up in your account? Or not?

> **It is possible to make all the money you want,
> from the things you most want to do.
> You have the power to design a life around what
> is important to you.**

The reason you haven't made more money or happiness so far is likely to be fairly straightforward. Because you don't think you can *Make Money, Be Happy*, or you are unable to take action (for a variety of reasons). Here are some positive statements and responses – do these responses seem familiar to you?

How do your attack thoughts compare to these?

My suggestion . . . Just deciding to *Make Money, Be Happy* could wake up something strong and determined within yourself. The part of you that wants more control, to feel better about yourself, to leave behind the swamps of debt or work frustration.

A possible response . . . *"Right, so just deciding to change makes it happen. Rubbish, everyone is trying hard, it's just incredibly difficult to be happy in your work, never mind earn lots of money at it."*

My suggestion . . . It is possible to make all the money you want, from the things you most want to do.

A possible response . . . *And pigs might fly. If I was born rich, maybe. That is just not applicable to my life.*

My suggestion . . . You have the power to design a life around what is important to you.

A possible response . . . *OK, now I'm bionic as well as multi-tasking, 24/7/365. I don't have time to think, never mind design a more fulfilling life!*

My suggestion . . . The reason you haven't made more money, or happiness so far is likely to be fairly straightforward. It is because you don't think you can *Make Money, Be Happy*, or you are unable to take action (for a variety of reasons).

A possible response . . . *Rubbish. I think about how to make money and get more fulfilment a lot, it's just that my boss and the hierarchy I work for have a different view. They tell me £20k and endless spreadsheets is* Make Money, Be Happy *bigtime!*

Attack thoughts. Like attack dogs, keen to savage first, be sorry later. What degree of ferocity did you encounter?

This is a confusing time (a little social context in a box)

Should life be as our parents knew it, with priority given to the secure job, steady progress and stability? Or is that suckerdom in these faster, more ambitious times?

Is it best, or naïve, to retain a debt of loyalty to the current boss? Should we design "portfolio" working lives, as the media suggest, gain portable skills, a mobile attitude and expect time out for travel and study? Is it only the rich that can create room to self-actualize and get the work–life balance right?

What about how rich or poor we feel? We are, in my view, at the ragged end of a social revolution which means no-one really knows the rules anymore. Apart from, keep working so you can keep buying – the perpetual motion of clever, adaptive capitalism. Consumer debt, some funded by home equity, means we never-never had it so good, even if the thing is broken before it's paid for. But with all this consumption, is there a growing "stress of stuff?" . The rural idyll lifestyle characterized by *The Good Life* attracts serious ratings.

And what about identity? We are urged to be globally mobile in terms of our 24/7 economic brands, but increasingly desire the comfort of a small team, customer proximity, local shops, kind communities. We are asked to be on call whenever the customer needs us to be, (yes of course I'm on the mobile next week, I'm only having a week off). The soul-sucking extension of clever capitalism or just a moan-yana UK workplace catching up with American-set standards of trade?

Questions swirl in what feels like a big, option-rich, fear-rich soup. What is the best strategy? You decide – hopefully on something that will *Make Money, Be Happy.*

One thing for sure. For those in the middle of all this, it is a confusing time.

Leisure

What is this life if, full of care,
We have no time to stand and stare?

No time to stand beneath the boughs,
And stare as long as sheep or cows:

No time to see, when woods we pass,
Where squirrels hide their nuts in grass:

No time to see, in broad daylight,
Streams full of stars, like skies at night:

No time to turn at Beauty's glance,
And watch her feet, how they can dance:

No time to wait till her mouth can
Enrich that smile her eyes began?

A poor life this if, full of care,
We have no time to stand and stare.

William Henry Davies, 1871–1940

What makes you happy?

> Life is a matter of passing the time enjoyably. There may be other things in life, but I've been too busy passing my time enjoyably, to think very deeply about them. Peter Cook, 1994

When I ask audiences "what is it about your job that makes you happy" I don't get many responses about pay. I get lots (even from the most revenue-driven corporate audiences) about feeling recognized for a job well done, being able to solve problems, being able to work in a close team, feeling supported and able to offer support to colleagues. Time and time again I expect to hear "bonustime " or "the car" but I just don't. Asked the same question, what might your answer be?

There is something of an urban myth about choosing work simply because it pays well. Or maybe it is easier to talk about the financial perks than about more personal aspects such as being recognized. Not sure. But even allowing for my biases(!) doesn't this suggest that something about human connection and challenge is more important than the material rewards? The good news is, it is possible to have both. In fact, the more connected they are, the better – as I hope to show through ten big ideas on how to *Make Money, Be Happy*.

Ten big ideas

The first big idea. **What makes you happy is the most effective route to making money.** Yes, that does mean the title might be the wrong way round. Thank you for noticing. It should be "be happy, make money". But that didn't sound right to me. Besides, I blame the parents. So, one foundation concept in this book is the link between fulfilling, purposeful work and income. This topic is explored in more detail on page 140.

Next one. Salaried income is not the same as wealth – even if you earn a lot of money each month. **Wealth equals assets.** An asset can be many things. A two-bed flat with lovely tenants, shares in a thriving organic farm, a trademarked idea, copyright on the Bond theme tune, a stud racehorse, a goose that lays golden eggs or all of the above. The key thing about an asset is its ability to create income without you needing to turn up, be there and be nice. You don't need to be there physically at all. Unlike making salaried income. Wealth happens slowly over time, when you choose to turn any surplus income – even a small amount – into assets. Those assets then create asset-based income – another stream of money separate to your salary in the form of rents, or dividends, or other financial returns.

Yes, I know the concept of surplus income is largely theoretical for many people. But for many rich individuals, the decision to create some surplus income, i.e. disposable money with debts under control, was a turning point in their lives. The default is to keep earning, spending, paying off debts every month, never ever getting ahead, and staying scared of anything (i.e. redundancy, long-term sickness) that cuts off the sole income stream. So that is why I put the concept of assets right here upfront.

> Happy the man, and happy he alone,
> He, who can call to-day his own:
> He who, secure within, can say,
> To-morrow do thy worst, for I have lived to-day.
> John Dryden, 1631–1700

In some ways relying on monthly income is like renting where you live, inasmuch as it can be great, but you can never be sure of the longevity of the arrangement. Your job could be gone next year, and your costs probably won't. In that way, salary-based income versus asset-based income is perhaps the difference between renting a lifestyle month-to-month and owning a life.

Number three. **Buy assets from the heart**. Only buy assets you care about. Many people don't consider assets at all because, like running the marathon, having children and stopping smoking, all that comes later. But what if investment could be enjoyable now? As with career strategy, you are more likely to be successful in asset building if you first define your values and most passionate interests. Then buy assets that will make you happy because they are an expression of what you believe in.

Of course you need to ensure good yield and financial performance – and there is lots of advice available to help you understand this. But don't ignore the potential to make money, or feel duty bound to buy investments you neither know nor care about, just because others do, or because finance pundits are busy putting forward this year's fabulous investment fad.

For example, if you are a social activist at heart, you could grow wealth from booming social enterprise firms and ethical financial investments. If your career is in music, consider investing in rare instruments, concert hall property developments or local recording studios. As a teacher, you might want to invest in ethical educational publishers, in educational software, in shared property ownership. There are as many investment opportunities as there are interests.

So if a stock market tracker fund or "buy-to-let" property doesn't grab you, you don't have to end the idea of asset ownership there. Go find profitable assets that also allow you to express your true values, and *Make Money, Be Happy*. The following models make the same point.

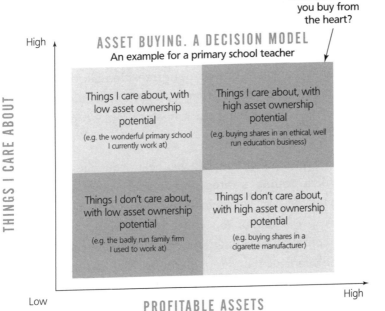

Asset decision model – one for you to consider:

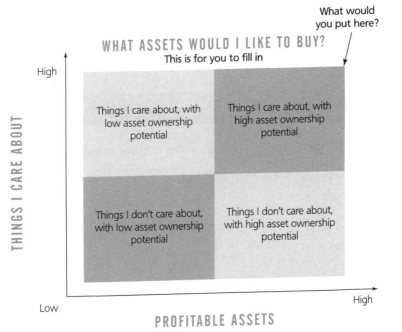

Big idea four. **We are all in transition. Even if you are in loads of debt, with a job that aches at soul level, you are still able to move your story forward.** It might be slow, but the key to your success could be to move slowly in the right direction. The concept of being in transition allows for a difficult starting point, and is simply an optimistic mindset. Better than giving up or staying stuck in some junky coping strategy. Much.

And now for number five. Did you hear about **the person who mistook a coping strategy for a life**? Here's how it goes. Trying for the best we could (*Make Money, Be Happy*) can seem too scary. Too full of obstacles. So, we settle for less, then create complicated coping strategies, designed to compensate for our fundamental disappointment. Coping strategies like rampant spending, or drinking (neither a pretty sight). Chasing status at work – even if you have to play bully. Coping strategies like owning lots of expensive gadget stuff and lording it over those who have less. More stuff is not happiness. *You deserve better. You deserve a happy, fulfilled and financially sound life.* No coping strategy can ever compensate for missing out on a life that makes you really happy.

Twelve ways to spot a coping strategy

1 You regularly spend money on treats, to cheer yourself up.

2 You get very irritated by people talking about plans for the future. The smarmy army.

3 You don't open lots of mail (including e-mail) because, well, who cares?

4 Your friends wonder why a lovely person like you gets so angry so often.

5 You're tired today, probably coming down with something again.

6 You find yourself playing games and online poker rather than doing that urgent thing for your colleagues.

7 Your new hobby gadget is your whole life – and you believe it was well worth the money.

8 You dread the end of your weekend/holiday/day off.

9 You've stopped listening to advice – thanks anyway.

10 You'd rather read horoscopes/car mags/the nearest phone book, than work on your CV.

11 Your family get their faces bitten off when they ask how the job is going.

12 You're too busy to think about this, right now – so leave it, OK?

The sixth big idea is this. **Just because you find what makes you happy, doesn't mean you'll make money, or vice versa. You need to actively manage both at the same time.** For the rest of the book, this gets called the dual strategy.

Seven. This book **encourages you to seek work which fulfils you**. Fulfilling work creates the capacity to work harder, learn faster, keep going even when things don't go well. To succeed even. And – major point – staying with something just for money won't even get you the money, longer term. What gets you the money is being the best, caring more, contributing more. Adding more value, creating newness, being unselfish. More of that and your story moves forward. You become a key player, niche, rare, prized, promoted. And precious. From precious you can choose to move to pricey. At pricey, you can afford assets. Assets allow you to move to even more fulfilling work. Or to the Riviera.

Eight. **Pain and frustration in your life are worth listening to.** Your career might have everything. The fulfilment, the finance, the frills and spills. Fantastic. However, if it doesn't, don't expect the sky to fly a personalized message showing you what you've got to do to change. You need to note the things that don't work, because every bit of dissatisfaction is trying to tell you something. Very wonderfully, your body and soul knows how to be healthy, even if your mind forgets from time to time. We feel pain for lots of good reasons. A finger in the fire starts to hurt, forcing you (a) to listen and make some changes or (b) to ignore it and over-ride the pain. A starved soul starts to carve some emptiness in your heart, forcing you (a) to listen and make some changes or (b) to create ever louder distractions and hope it goes away. The pain you might be feeling in your life is data. It is telling you something about things you need to change. So don't look away – acknowledge pain and frustration for the messengers they can be.

The ninth big idea. It seems to me that an increasing number of individuals feel under siege – from more job pressure, more debt. And, at the same time, are expected to have more ambition, more aspiration, more professional qualifications. Oh yes, and look celeb-pretty on a tenth of their haircare budget. Go away and give my head peace. I feel under siege myself most days. The adverts tell me my car doesn't have any va va whatsit, my holiday choice is unsexy. And don't even talk about my choice of personal haircare products. It seems everything about me is in desperate need of an upgrade. But hold on. What if I have to be persuaded that I am not good enough, simply to ensure the marketeers meet their sales targets? **What would happen if we all decided we're good enough as we are, not broken, not needing another Saturday morning fix from the shops?** You and I are fine as we are. Even if every fibre in our credit cards tells us different. How would that belief change your life?

Maybe our own sense of purpose, happiness and prosperity could guide our actions, lead us from here to someplace happier, rather than be deafened by the daily roar of buying and spending. Oh, and the accompanying worries about financial survival.

The way things are just doesn't seem right. Instead of all of us following the twenty-first century religion (belief in struggling to have it all, all the time) how about another view? We are not born into this abundant, beautiful world to scrape through, courtesy of a high street loan. There is a gap in today's market for hope. Do you believe you deserve to, and could, *Make Money, Be Happy*? Could your splendid humanity insist that you claim a life on your own terms? Not those of your boss, the mortgage company, MasterCard or anyone else. *Those hopes and dreams inside you are important. You are important.*

Last big idea (for now) is **It's down to you**. Although you, your best mate and no doubt the Chairman would prefer soft victimhood to active engagement with life's big scary bits, **taking personal responsibility for what happens in your life is the foundation of any personal success**. This includes mine. One big step was to narrow the list of people in charge of my life to one (me) and work out what I could do. Not expecting my employer to do something first, or my bank, or members of my family. The better questions were – how can I change? How can I become the one to congratulate or, at times, blame for what is going on?

And that perspective made a huge difference.

> **The best way to predict the future is to invent it.**
> Alan Kay

So far so big.

Leaving all that to one side for a minute, can I ask you something? Do you ever feel detached from your life? Like you are working on something that doesn't mean a great deal to you? If yes, can I suggest that these problems may have arisen for one reason. It could be because you have taken the chicken option.

The chicken option

Now. Throughout this book I will describe the parallel path you can, at any time, choose to take. The path of least resistance (and reward) which shall be called the way of the chicken. Do not, please, plead for the right to substitute some other word, creature or way because my mind is made up. "Chicken" is going to be the name you get called unless you start working with me. Bossy bully stuff, right? Yes. But I would argue, for your higher good.

You see I only just stepped down from full-time chickenhood myself. I kept my pecker up, didn't try to fly and ate the strange stuff my boss threw my way for many years. Then I got clucky. Sorry, lucky. Life as a chicken was starting to sicken me; cooped up in the nice company that looked after me was starting to feel harder than a braver, non-chicken (let's say human) route. Now I am not saying that each office job is a battery farm. Not at all. In many organizations freedom, openness and customer focus is the rule. It just wasn't for me, then. So I picked up my head, made a dash for the door, and really didn't know what to expect outside the boss's domain. I just knew I couldn't wait for something big to hatch, and get taken away from me, any longer. Like most of my good ideas. And by escaping chickenhood I slowly learned how to create a life with more satisfaction, as well as income.

So, dear reader, you get the best use out of the cover price if you come to this page ready to move your own story forward. Even better when you get your senses lined up to take action, after some *self* investment on these pages. Action is very good. If you hit the brake on action every time you have a good idea, or if you reward every look above the noise of routine with a big "I'll be fine just as I am – let's see", believe this, I am going to refer you, regularly, to the chicken option. A life scratching round looking at the things you want to change. Again. Now and again rewarded by good feed or some new rooster to raise morale; some (though not me) would say a poultry reward, versus a life of human fulfilment. Which is the other option on offer.

That's all I mean by the chicken option. But, hey. You bought this book, and very few chickens have done. I believe.

As that was a tough little section to read, let me soften the news with some big questions, answered.

Why am I here? Answer. Your parents made you.

You see. You have, in me, a trusted adviser on life's big questions. And also, there will be more on avoiding chickenhood later. Could life get any better?

Ah. The purpose of this book in just one question.

Great expectations

A pessimist sees the difficulty in every opportunity; an optimist sees the opportunity in every difficulty. Winston Churchill

An optimist is a guy who has never had much experience. Don Marquis, 1927

02

Do you still have them?

I mean great expectations about your own future. What do you forecast? How about a glorious set of years, strewn with happiness and fulfilment, sunny days full of love and fun. Moving from a state of less to a state of more money. From less to more happy.

Do you see what I mean about transition? How does that sound? And, if I can be blunt, do you feel that positive transition is on or off the agenda? I'd like to help you believe this kind of life is your agenda. Perhaps there needs to be a little supportive engagement with a few areas, but hey, no reason to lose sight of the fact you can *Make Money, Be Happy*. The great expectation we'll look at right now. I'd like to offer two approaches to help you *Make Money, Be Happy*. The first is this.

Purposeful profit: one way to Make Money, Be Happy

First step

Work out what makes you happy and find someone who will gladly pay you to do it. Ensure you have the skills, real desire and are in the right town. Then do it.

Do it as an employee or do it as a freelancer. Do it part-time or do it full-time. Do it as a first job or do it after your 70th birthday. Do it so your income reflects how happy you make other people. Do it through products and services, do it as creative advice, do it as a way of changing the world or as a way of changing your bank balance first.

Second step

When money starts to flow from work that makes you happy, start to manage the financial side more accurately. First of all see off any unhelpful debts – highest interest first.

Third step

Use any surplus income (and yes I know this is not easy to get hold of) to buy an asset. What is an asset? See page 27. You may not like the look of most commonly proferred assets – and this is where finding your personal preference is critical. The key is to buy assets from the heart. You have to care about your portfolio – doing it just for money is as daft in asset building as it is in career building. Or, perhaps I should say, it can be done, but it is not likely to be the most successful strategy.

> As your career strategy, so your asset building strategy. Aim for work that fulfils you. Only buy assets you really care about.

If you want to build assets, choose those assets based on what makes you happy. Identify assets which continue an existing interest.

For example, if you are interested in social change, buy into firms making ethical profits. Find a firm or firms that make money furthering a cause that you are personally passionate about – whether it is recycling, worker rights in developing countries, green energy and so on. (Sources include EIRIS, *Directory of Social Change*, Footse4Good, Triodos, *Ethical Consumer* mag, *Corporate Watch*.) Get hold of some annual reports so that you have a good understanding of a number of investment options. Find out which companies to back and either buy shares direct (ask your bank how they can help you do this) or use an investment vehicle such as an ISA. Become a social investor, with your financial best interests at heart. The ethical investment sector has become a huge growth area.

If you are interested in vintage cars, well, provided you do the research, the right piece of motoring history could become another investment vehicle. Ho, ho, ho. If you are interested in learning more about the workings of the share market, join or start an investment club. You don't have to hand over your surplus income to an anonymous pension fund or investment. There are more options.

> **What do you love? That's the first question when it comes to building assets.**

Purpose-linked assets are the only route I know to big wealth. Unconnected assets soon become part of the stress of stuff – a hassle rather than something you enjoy. And you start paying advisers to sort them out – which isn't always a good idea.

This is where I feel duty bound to point out that the value of assets go up and down – not, interestingly, based on their value, but based on that most intangible of measures, market confidence. Assets with high demand keep their value. Assets with lower demand lose theirs – regardless of the workmanship, the history, the condition. Market confidence and demand drive price more than intrinsic worth any old day. The market and quantity of buyer interest determines price, not the cost of production or calibre of the management team. For proof, just look at the boom and bust of stockmarket cycles. During each boom, whether it be

Dutch tulips in the mid-seventeenth century or dot.com firms at the end of the last, share prices become inflated beyond belief, with no discernable difference in the quality of the product. Why? Because a surfeit of investors created an atmosphere of extreme market confidence about future profits. The fact that the internet business model was, shall we say, flawed, was overlooked because investors believed they had to be in at the start or else risk losing a fortune. Demand can cause investors to forget the basics about how business works, but their herd-like enthusiasm has a tangible, real impact on prices. Dot.com came and went, and we're probably onto the next one. China anyone?

So there is a lesson about assets – they only retain value where demand exists. And if your investment loses market confidence, for the most illogical of reasons, you could lose your money.

Without assets, you and I have to rely on our income. The reassuring bank fix each month which means we can live our lives. Income usually requires you to turn up, be there and be nice. And sometimes you may not want to. Salary (income, wages) can and usually does increase with time and value investment, such as specialist study but they generally won't buy the rights to your time. Income simply allows you to rent a lifestyle. And, as with any kind of rental, the decision about when to change things is not always yours. The market decides whether your job is most profitably placed in London, or Bangalore, or Shanghai. The boss decides whether your performance meets the necessary standards. The department is being reduced. Sorry. Have an outplacement counsellor.

Consider owning, rather than renting the time in your day, the weeks in your year, the years in your time on earth. Surely something worth investigating? Your ownership of assets which create income without your day-to-day input is your passport out of employeedom – and I completely understand if that passport is unnecessary in your case because you love being part of an organization. It is fine, as long as the choice has been made. And, by the way, what is your multiple income strategy just in case the organization decides the feeling ain't mutual?

My view on how to create purposeful profit? Don't assume you are income dependent until you have checked out the alternative. Be open to the idea of financial independence through assets.

Some thinking, research and discussion with your loved ones about your financial future are not financially risky activities. Keeping your head in the sand probably is.

Figure out what you care about, buy assets, from the heart, where you have a personal connection and always do the research. Remember your goal is to move from being income dependent to asset rich. And plan to grow your number of income producing assets into a (you may have heard this phrase before) balanced portfolio. Which means some high risk, some low risk investments.

> Wealth = the total value of your assets, not the amount of your income.

Any money that only comes in as a direct result of you turning up, is probably a high risk money making strategy, so making the transition from income-based living to a mixture of asset- and income-based living is really a very good idea. And I am prepared to convince you if you don't agree just now!

Now, you may argue that some people get very rich working for an income. Long-term employees who move up the hierarchy can get very rich. Senior public servants and consultants get rich. That is true, and is another way to build assets. Those senior people have invested time, which like compound interest will increase in value exponentially if the single focus is kept. Say, dear reader, you are in your 25th year. If, like Lord Browne at BP or Niall Fitzgerald at Unilever, you choose to spend the 25 years creating a network, single industry expertise, internal process and system competency, don't you think you'd be worth a lot to the company? The lifer (as this single-career professional often gets called) is often very wealthy. But only when they add professional assets to their CV (more on building professional career assets is shown on the asset ladder model on page 97).

So, before you decide on this life-long commitment as a strategy, you need to ask yourself a tough question . . .

Does my career make a profit?

Jobs may not create wealth unless you are prepared to go with the long-term investment of self (i.e. turn up everyday, stay loyal to the long-term plan if not the current brand) and go for the big promotions. This is a common misunderstanding. If you are not keen (or able, or likely) to get promoted, growing assets rather than seeking to grow income from the day job can be a much better strategy to make money. Your job could be an expensive option, given the opportunity costs associated with doing that full-time, rather than something else that grows assets. If you were to fast-forward time in your current job by five years, and add 5% salary increase each year, plus bonus, will you be much more prosperous? Or does the increased cost of living eat away any raise year-on-year? What do you feel about that scenario?

Your work may not create profit. Many jobs don't. Many jobs generate a monthly credit into the bank account, much of which

> The ratio of household debt to income has soared from less than 100% in 1997 to around 135% now, with mortgage lending by banks growing by 10% a quarter and unsecured lending in the form of credit cards, loans and overdrafts by 13% a quarter over the past year. *Financial Stability Review*, the Bank of England, June 2004

goes straight out on monthly debt repayments (like the mortgage, which is still a debt, albeit a less scary debt, i.e. a secured loan[2]). The monthly cheque can also create a substantial, if temporary high, a sense of affluence which can cloud other judgements. In my mind, it usually runs like "How can I be in debt when I just got £... into my bank account?" I imagine my monthly cheque to be an all conquering hero, cancelling out other larger sums owed, by its sheer magnificence. And perhaps, because I remember how much work it took to get there.

If making some kind of profit is important to you, this book has some ideas on creating money, either as part of, or separate to, your career. Careers and money are usually grouped together, but I would argue that isn't always correct. Some careers produce debt. Some careers produce erratic money. Some careers produce regular profit. The thing is, you and I do not get

[2]My subjective view on less vs more scary debt: a mortgage is a less scary debt because the building society own your house until you have paid off the capital they have loaned to you for its purchase. The mortgage is a secured loan – secured against the property itself. So you are not criminal, or bankrupt if you cannot pay back the mortgage, though the building society will take possession of what was once your home. A more scary debt is credit card and consumer debt, not secured against any assets. Without security against assets, your good reputation and credit record becomes the price paid for failure to repay. Bankruptcy is the end of that particular road.

> They say hard work never hurt anybody,
> but I figure why take the chance? Ronald Reagan

any guidance on this strange state of affairs, from anyone, anywhere. Which is a bit of a swizz. Many careers get launched on the basis of an increasing wage over time. And while jam tomorrow is fine in theory, in practice the stress of debt puts many people in a jam, today.

How then, to make sure money making doesn't get left behind while career making?

Ten suggested ways to earn more – from an employee point of view

1 Understand why your employer invests your salary in you. In particular, understand value added (and the value of your work) by figuring out how your role meets customer needs and expectations. (Scary question – if you don't have a customer, internal or external, perhaps you don't add value?)

2 Understand the financial priorities in the organization.

3 Insist on having visible, measurable objectives even if the firm doesn't automatically provide them.

4 Make sure your pay is linked to meeting objectives. Negotiate your pay based on benchmark data for comparable jobs and where possible negotiate for linked share options so you start to grow assets.

6 Be a broker – cross-fertilize ideas, rapport, even cash between different parts of the business and within your industry. Ethically, of course!

7 Understand the value chain (and the most lucrative bits) and move up it.

8 Gain profile by solving high-value problems or creating new ideas.

9 Have a portfolio of tools and methodologies to make change happen – it is a crucial part of nearly every job.

10 Create a six-month savings buffer, or better still asset-based sources of income so you can walk if necessary.

The corporate lifer is a human form of compound interest, constantly re-investing interest back into one focused area. This still seems to be the standard career model, even with the hype about portfolio workers and workplace revolutions. What has happened, however, is a rise in flexible working, causing a similar increase in personal decisions to be made about whether to work from home, part-time, temporary, or in shift work. This pattern, in my view, is one of the factors leading to more and wider thinking about the purpose and timing of our careers. The corporate lifer who happened to be male had no chance of a career break, or working from home, or paternity leave thirty years ago. Slowly, employers realized that a motivated workforce required that they open the doors of the workplace to let people out now and again. And through those newly open doors, the light of many more career options has come streaming in for the rest of us.

In 1901 women were more likely than men to work from home but in 2003 the situation was reversed, and 14 per cent of men worked from home compared with 8 per cent of women. Almost one-quarter of men working part-time in 2003 said that they did so because they could afford not to work full-time, whereas 41 per cent of women working part-time wanted to spend more time with the family.

Trish McOrmond, *Labour Market Trends*, vol. 112, no. 1, 8 January 2004

It does seem that more of us are choosing a varied, multi-focal career path rather than as an employee loyal to one brand for several decades. Many excellent books exist (such as *The Rules of Work* by Richard Templar) to help if you are keen on the single career path. If you think that your career is more likely to be divided between a number of different interests, asset building is really the much more robust financial strategy.

Here is an example. Two best friends start their careers at around the same time. One, Steven, works in finance for a local authority. The other, Tina, works as cabin crew for a large airline. They both progress through several promotions and, after five years, take stock. Steven has realized that his job doesn't energize or even interest him much anymore. Looking up the hierarchy, he doesn't want the bosses' bosses' job. Looking at sideways moves or a jump into the private sector leaves him equally underwhelmed. He is worried that as time goes by, he becomes more emotionally detached from his work, which has a bad effect on his performance, and which means he becomes less valuable as an employee. He feels stuck.

Tina, on the other hand, loves her work, loves the lifestyle and the considerable challenge of leading a crew and keeping passengers happy during each long-haul flight. She has learned about airline industry management and won internal awards for customer care. You might suggest Tina is an all round high flyer. The work that she loves to do is well paid, which means she has found purposeful profit, her own way to *Make Money, Be Happy*.

Steven on the other hand needs to invest a bit of time in his own dual strategy. First to identify and major on parts of the job that he does still enjoy. Then to work out the link between those, most personally satisfying parts of his work and the overall value added for the organization, so that he can negotiate with his boss.

> **Employers are delighted (usually) when an employee works out the overall purpose of the organization, and negotiates for a more interesting piece of the action.**

For example, Steven loves running workshops to help small local enterprises become more financially aware, but this is only a small part of his community development role. Most of his time is spent producing reports and evaluating existing performance. By helping his boss see how valuable those workshops are – in terms of meeting the department goals for the year – Steven could negotiate more time doing the work he prefers. Hopefully this will bring greater energy and interest to his role while he evaluates other career options. (Or maybe, after this, he won't feel so detached from his job anyway!)

But assuming he still wants a change, Steven's next dual strategy task is to identify and invest in some assets to produce income. That way, should he decide to retrain, or reduce his hours so that he can work part-time at something more fulfilling, the gap in employment salary will be compensated for by income from assets. The dual strategy for Steven is to find a personally satisfying way to add value in the job, while looking for assets he can buy to produce longer-term income outside of the day job. With an asset producing regular income (let's say surplus monthly income of £400 after costs from a buy-to-let flat), Steven can work part-time and study part-time. He has the choice to retrain, or take up another path entirely, secure in the knowledge that his assets will produce income to pay for day-to-day bills and living costs.

Now back to you. Perhaps a good moment to think about choices you have right here and right now.

EXERCISE

What would your dual strategy look like?

QUESTIONS	ANSWERS
1. Which three areas of your job do you enjoy most? For example, is it the problem solving, or the team parts or the pure data analysis? Which?	
2. Which of these are most likely to make your customers or users happy? Why? (See the model on page 59 for more on this.)	
3. Is that valuable to your employer? In what way?	
4. Can you use that value to negotiate an increase in the quantity of work that you most enjoy? (Working on the simple idea that you will feel more fulfilled by work that you enjoy.)	
5. Who do you need to talk to, or what action could you take very quickly to kick the process off?	

Next stage – your money situation.

QUESTIONS	ANSWERS
6. How much money do you need each month to live comfortably? Excludes yachts and big trips, includes debt payments and usual fun.	
7. Based on that amount, what monthly income do you need to earn to increase your current options? For example, so that you could work part-time, retrain, take time off for travel?	
8. How much extra per month – £...............	
9. What drives you? What evidence exists in your life about your passions, interests, dreams? This is key to successful asset building – buying assets from the heart.	
10. What would your friends and family say to that last question? (Asking them is always interesting.)	
11. What assets have most appeal? Which of those is most likely to create regular income? (See page 29 for more on this – reminder opposite)	

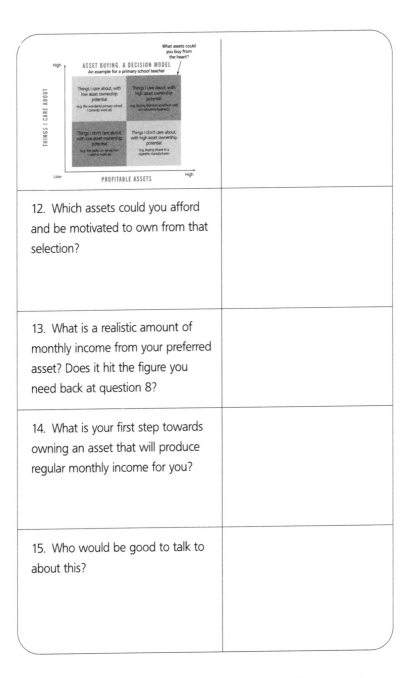

ASSET BUYING. A DECISION MODEL
An example for a primary school teacher

What assets could you buy from the heart?

THINGS I CARE ABOUT

High

Things I care about, with low asset ownership potential

(e.g. the wonderful primary school I currently work at)

Things I care about, with high asset ownership potential

(e.g. buying shares in an ethical, well run education business)

Things I don't care about, with low asset ownership potential

(e.g. the badly run family firm I used to work at)

Things I don't care about, with high asset ownership potential

(e.g. buying shares in a cigarette manufacturer)

Low

PROFITABLE ASSETS

High

---

12. Which assets could you afford and be motivated to own from that selection?

13. What is a realistic amount of monthly income from your preferred asset? Does it hit the figure you need back at question 8?

14. What is your first step towards owning an asset that will produce regular monthly income for you?

15. Who would be good to talk to about this?

Quick thought. Did you skip that last bit? Well, it is understandable. A first instinct might be to deny that more choice exists in your life right now. Much better to hide under some all-encompassing alibi, for example, "I would but others are stopping me". Or "now just isn't the right time". Or "I really don't know what I want to do". Those phrases echo nothing more persuasive than fear – specifically your fear of the new – they really don't count as good enough reasons to give up. Especially given the successes you've already had when you've managed to get past your natural nerves. Fear may not be your best buddy here.

Just for now, imagine your dual strategy couldn't fail. Imagine that there is an easy door to the work that fulfils you, creating both having money and happiness. If you could first of all start thinking in a less limited way. So if you decided to look away, please could I ask you to read the exercise again, and just ask yourself, "what am I scared of here?". No one need see your answers. Just allow yourself the idea that you can improve things slowly, but surely.

Money basics (a guide for those who've been doing more interesting things)

Perhaps now is a reasonably good time to talk about some universal rules. In nature there is ebb and flow. In terms of income and expenditure, the same is true. There will be times in your life when you earn more, and times when you earn less. Another universal rule is gravity. What goes up must come down, in financial markets as in apples. There is a cycle of bull and bear markets.[3] The value of your investments will gently yo-yo up and down over the years, and if you want, you can make money by understanding the movement of financial markets. After all, the City of London does. Allowing that these cycles exist is a

---

[3]A bull market is where stock prices are generally rising – a time of recovery and growth. A bear market is where stock prices are generally falling – a time of reduced growth and recession.

good idea. The alternative is to blame yourself if earnings flatten out, or go down. There are people who have become wildly frustrated during times of less income, less bonus, reduced property prices and/or higher living costs. They come to expect that their income will keep rising each year – but national economies and financial markets follow the same natural rules. And I would suggest it is the same for your personal economy. So maybe it is useful to think there is an ebb and flow of money, natural ups and downs along the road to prosperity. And save yourself the indigestion.

My business cycle – an exercise

Building on the idea of natural rules in finance, economists believe business moves in cycles of faster or slower growth. The four stages are recovery, peak, slowdown and trough. Most personal economies follow this pattern – or do they? What is your experience? This exercise will help you map your personal economy to help answer that question.

Draw a line starting with your first paid work. When was that, and how much did you earn? How much do you remember spending? Yes – a very hard question!

Chart the changes at summary level, by year and with some brief annotation. Looking back at your career so far, what would you say the pattern has been in terms of income and expenditure?

Date (e.g. when I started work) . . . . Now

Income

Spending

Are you finance friendly or finance phobic? Please tick.

QUESTION	TRUE	UNTRUE
1. I am determined to live within my means.		
2. I check my bank account each month and make sure it all balances out.		
3. I pay my bills on time.		
4. I don't have debts apart from my mortgage.		
5. I regularly save money.		
6. I only use credit cards and store cards when I know I can clear the balance before high interest charges apply. Or in emergencies.		
7. I feel good about my finances generally.		
8. I know how much I spend each month on personal and work expenses.		
9. I pay my credit and store cards in full each month.		

QUESTION	TRUE	UNTRUE
10 I always make sure I have the right amount of cash with me for day-to-day needs.		
11. I pay my taxes on time.		
12. I have a good financial adviser who knows my financial goals and supports me.		
13. I know what to do with any surplus money.		
14. I always keep some money (at least a month's wages) for unexpected expenses.		
15. I am saving to put a three-month salary buffer in the bank, in case I want to change career direction or travel.		

Scores

Count how many times you ticked "True".

Up to 7 ticks in the "True" column

You know it yourself – your financial acumen is fairly limited. Perhaps this is phobia, perhaps it is because you have never needed to become knowledgeable. Either way, you will appreciate the improvement with just the smallest amount of new awareness and application.

Between 7 and 14 ticks

You are a mixture – could improve in some areas but probably not in financial duress. If you were to re-read the questions, which area strikes you as being most urgent to tackle? Perhaps just focus on one or two areas to begin with.

More than 14 ticks

Finance friendly to say the least. You could congratulate your-self, maybe by sharing a bit of know-how on how you've managed it so far!

We'll return to finances later. I just wanted you to consider how you feel about finance so that your insight can bubble away while we look at your expectations about "money" and "happy".

A different kind of expectation

> Discover the work that fulfils you, find the best marketplace for it and go *Make Money, Be Happy*. Then use any surplus to create assets – once again based on what you love to do.

Just like that? No way can it be that simple.

OK, I hear you, your life is rough, tough and full of stressful stuff. And that is normal. Look out the window and see how much – or rather how little – happiness exists, visibly. Get real.

Alright. Maybe I make the case for optimism in the face of over-whelming evidence to the contrary. But what about having some views that support your transition to money and happiness rather than views that don't serve you? For example, what if your life might not have to be a struggle?

Is there any rule that says money can't be made from work that feels fulfilling, satisfying, purposeful? Don't think so. Is there evidence that motivation and personal commitment to your work makes a difference to performance? Seems so. Are you prepared to open your mind to the option of making money through happiness? Then good. This is the first way to *Make Money, Be Happy*. Your happiness as competitive advantage – a way to activate change in your life. If you like.

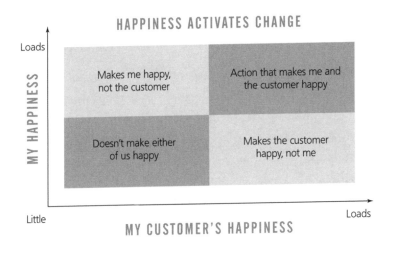

What parts of your job fit into that top right hand corner?,

There is, of course, an alternative. You could choose a career that doesn't make you happy. Or deny how you feel most days and remain locked into a career that made you happy, once. You could compromise, pretend, collude. Squeeze your uniqueness into some job that doesn't fit and watch for the results – all sorts of sore heart behaviour. What do I mean by sore heart behaviour? Well, living a life that is low on authentic happiness, high on coping strategies. For example, over-consumption, under-achievement. For most people, a main dish of coping strategy usually comes with a side order of low self-esteem and conversational over-defensiveness. In my experience, if someone has to proclaim loudly how totally tremendous their life is, chances are that person decided to sit on their disappointment rather than get up off it and do something. I remember doing it myself – and yes I thought it was convincing and true rather than transparent insecurity at the time. Oh yes.

Of course, there are many times when it is just hard to know what is happening. For example when you are just getting into or out of a new job or career change – that can be hard as well. How can you tell which situation you inhabit right now? How, in the middle of all the busyness etc., can you see if you're locked into something less than you deserve or living your full potential?

One way is to understand whether you are waiting for the next thing. Do you find yourself living for later, perhaps wishing time away with phrases like "one day nearer Friday", "one month 'til I go away", "nearly Xmas". This is a never-never land, and you are in danger of skimming through precious years, waiting for something to change. Waiting for the next thing to happen means missing this present moment – and this present moment holds all the power. If you can feel and believe you have all you need right now, life can very quickly feel much, much better than that – and you probably know it is you who has to change it. So is it true of you – do you find yourself waiting for later?

A career that doesn't fit, which causes you to live in never-never land also brings the need for coping strategies (as I mentioned earlier). Now these are really expensive. The over-consumption, "buy it for a treat" behaviours that can arise from workplace frustration are also, ironically, a big reason why so many of us get into debt. But more on that later on. In my experience, sort out the big questions first, then the smaller ones will sort themselves out.

> **Doing something blah for enough money for a car? That is not your best or only career option.**

A job which is not right for you just won't make you as much money as finding something that animates, thrills and deserves you. How do I know? Because, dear reader, I lived it, not just read about it. Call me over-experienced at unsuitable jobs, most of which I took simply because I didn't know enough about myself to argue for something better.

Typical scene. Working on something I didn't enjoy, so didn't work hard at. With others who seemed to (somehow) really enjoy it. I would try for a while, and give my bosses cause for hope. Then give up again. All the while, lying to myself, giving it 'til Xmas, 'til summer. Months of 9–5 spent trying to make my unworkable job work, evenings and weekend taking pent-up frustrations out on myself and anyone unfortunate to be around me. During one particularly unhappy time, I shredded good friendships, turned an occasional social drink into a must have now drink, couldn't sleep, gained or sometimes (er, once actually) lost weight. Bought huge quantities of shoes, navy blue suits (why?), handbags and sunglasses. Every lunchtime spent shopping. A variety of all consuming (literally) coping strategies meant I spent as much as I earned and I was still miserable.

Now, I recently gave up the habit of hanging onto every stinging regret, though I freely admit to lots of poor career choices, earlier on. How many? How long have you got?

Things have become easier since I figured out that, at each stage of my life I was just doing the best I could at the time, with the information I had at the time. Why has this made life easier?

Well, I no longer re-run painful images and upset myself about things I can't change. I spend less time remembering my earlier mistakes because that simply won't help me enjoy my life today, and I've realized each one of us has a choice about being imprisoned by past errors or letting them go. I feel really strongly about that bit, probably because I've wasted so many afternoons paralysed by guilt about how useless I've been that morning. You and I do the best we can at the time – so if you have a habit of self-walloping over earlier mistakes, just be kinder. You were doing your best; so how about you give yourself the chance to use today to make things happen, not lose it because of what has gone before.

> The past doesn't have any right to rule the present – for me or for you.

So this idea of *Make Money, Be Happy* represents 25 years of experience over 11 different jobs. And, thank God, my life is prosperous and happy just now – hence this strong desire to write up the lessons. Dear reader, this might save you time, and make you happier, and richer, faster.

13 jobs . . . 25 years

1 Marine cargo claims adjuster, aged 15.

2 Media advertising sales rep.

3 Operations clerk, investment bank (big US firm).

4 Full-time social activist (e.g. Greenham Common women's peace camp), aged 21.

5 Running a newsagents (in Marylebone, London).

6 Community radio outreach worker, aged 25.

7 Secretary, aged 28.

8 IT project manager and MBA student (for BT plc).

9 Leadership development consultant (freelance).

10 Management consultant (director, Holistic Management Ltd), aged 34.

11 Charity founder (Magic Breakfast) providing healthy breakfast foods to schools.

12 Author and conference speaker.

13 Social entrepreneur (Magic Outcomes providing social leadership development based in primary schools, all profits to Magic Breakfast), now aged 42.

I feel tired just looking at that. Thankfully it doesn't include the many educational tangents or never-to-be-used qualifications gained en route. Let's just say that if you need a sound engineer with good working knowledge of logistics IT, who also knows how to organize a newspaper round, I am your gal.

I hope this brief biography proves that purposeful profit is a fairly robust approach, in that it can apply to most individuals. Does this approach vary according to profession or age or gender or birthplace? Nope. Doesn't matter if the thing that makes you happy is nursing the sick or being a banker to the very wealthy. The same principle applies. Find out what makes you happy, then find a way to make it pay. Trust in yourself, taking action based on your real values isn't the easiest road

good shape. Get over the fact that your main choice of work may not also be your main provider of cash. It is OK.

The dual strategy means yours won't be a life of hellish poverty even if you spend 40 hours a week recording Beatles' cover versions, using your nan's spaniel on lead vocals. Some might say you'd deserve it, but this is a non-judgemental kind of book. While humming along to the howling, you'd have devised clever ways to earn money. Income from related skills, used imaginatively. Or income from assets, such as property. Those royalties from *A Hard Dogs Night* may well come rolling in, but just in case, it might be an idea to do some jobbing sound recording in the local studio or radio station. A feature of dual strategy income work is that while it may not feel fabulous, it does enable you to meet your day-to-day costs which could lead to more of the fabulous stuff.

You may need to fund your fulfilment separately for a year while training or you may need to fund it forever. You can create a dual strategy to meet whatever the timescale or whatever your income needs. You will need to acquire some financial nous and you will need to have some self-awareness about the beliefs and behaviours that can trip you up. But that might feel like a fair trade for a life you love.

> When what you love to do isn't going to find a buyer in the marketplace, find a way to earn money regardless. Whatever you do, don't give up on your dreams.

Now might be a reasonably good time to consider the way you think about your career, and life generally. The strategy you choose is going to depend on some of your answers to this gentle set of questions.

Please answer "true" or "false" to the following.

1 Most people postpone a fulfilling life until after the mortgage is paid off.
True or false?

2 Only those born rich can afford to do cool stuff which doesn't pay well.
True or false?

3 The only career option is to work hard at whatever job you end up in.
True or false?

4 Few really know what to do for a living. We all take a guess early on and hope for the best.
True or false?

How many did you answer true?

How many false?

If you answered true to more than two of those, you will want some serious convincing about my hypothesis that life can be better. I imagine that you have got this far, with ever straining incredulity. Some sympathy, but – let me guess. This *Make Money, Be Happy* thing doesn't work for you. Because . . . why? Why won't either of the two approaches so far work for you?

A reminder of the two approaches:

Purposeful profit

1 Discover the work that fulfils you. Find people who will pay you to do it (the best marketplace). Go *Make Money, Be Happy*.

Dual strategy

2 Discover the work that fulfils you. There isn't a marketplace, so you fund your fulfilment through other financial methods. Go *Make Money, Be Happy.*

Just get the reasons down now. The first approach won't work for me, because . . . .

. . . .

. . . .

. . . .

. . . .

. . . .

. . . .

. . . .

The second approach won't work for me because . . . .

. . . .

. . . .

. . . .

. . . .

. . . .

. . . .

Did you write any of the following reasons? Or variations. If you did, tick the nearest one.

The purposeful profit approach won't work because:

- ▦ I don't know what I want to do.
- ▦ Even if I did, I don't know what you mean by "find a market-place".
- ▦ I haven't got any money.
- ▦ I don't know how much I need to live on.
- ▦ I don't know what my skills are worth.
- ▦ What if I try and it all goes wrong?

- People like me don't go after fulfilment.
- I am in debt so I can't do anything other than stay here.
- This isn't a good time for me to change anything.
- I am not able to choose, because I just can't right now.

The dual strategy approach won't work because:

- All the reasons above.

Plus . . .

- I am not artistic or creative.
- I don't know anyone who is.
- My family/girlfriend/boyfriend/dog/boss/parents/neighbours/cat/ classmates won't understand.
- I am scared.
- I don't understand finance so how can I work out how much I need?
- I don't know what I would do for the income part of it.

The good news is, if you ticked any of the above, you are in the right place because this is stuff you are going to learn to overcome. Learning about it is not the same as doing something about it, so the book also contains some ideas for you to try out.

My own dual strategy

For most of my early career I had a kind of 9 to 5 amnesia, remembering who I was only after work and during weekends. During office hours I made sure I was the person most likely to keep the job first and foremost – not really true to myself. Somewhere along the line I found a way to be myself at work, to use the things I cared about out of hours to fuel my learning and effort inside the job. The alignment worked like magic. Suddenly I could link what made me happy – people being well treated,

BEHAVIOURS	TRUE	FALSE
17. Everyone I know is just like me, struggling to make a decent living.		
18. I usually follow advice from friends and family, even though they've been wrong in the past. But who else can I listen to?		
19. I've got loads of stuff, some of it is probably clutter. But why get rid of old things, when they might come in handy in the future?		
20. I would like to have a few words with the people who are responsible for what happens in my life. They're not doing a particularly good job.		
21. If I ever have money, it tends to go quickly, and I never know where.		
Now add up and write the total number of ticks in each column.		

Scores

First of all, count the number of ticks in the "True" column.

Up to 7 ticks

Sounds like you could be an optimist with a few doubts – you have a strong foundation for *Make Money, Be Happy*. Take a look at the ticks you entered under the "True" column and consider where those beliefs may have come from. They certainly are not serving your happiness just now – so these are likely to be the areas of greatest discomfort and stress in your life right now. So what did you learn – what would you most like to aim for? And, yes, I would recommend doing the questionnaire with someone who knows you!

Might you be in the top-left or bottom-right-hand corner of the four states diagram on page ix?

Between 7 and 14 ticks

Life possibly feels hard, without a clear direction or allies. You've probably got your defences up a lot of the time to safeguard against more hurt. You may feel let down, disappointed by how things have gone so far. If you notice the ticks under the "false" column, these represent the parts of your life that are working, which you do feel confident about. If you are in this category, the most pressing work is likely to be on resolving debt and confidence issues, and realizing that you are more in control than you think. What strikes you as the most damaging belief – one that holds you back?

By the way, how would the questionnaire go with someone who knows you? Same answers? Perhaps you could try it.

Are you in the bottom-left-hand corner on the four states diagram on page ix?

If you ticked "True" to less than 7 questions and ticked "False" to more than 7

If you found those questions difficult, or you are unsure perhaps ask someone to go through the questionnaire with you. Or try again when you're in a different mood.

Where are you now?

> A tree as big around as you can reach starts with a small seed; a thousand mile journey starts with one small step. Lao-tse

> What we call our future is the shadow which our past throws in front of us. Marcel Proust, 1918

03

In this chapter, the idea is to help you get a really good view of your current situation and priorities. You may have figured out which of the four states most closely describes your life. If not, it might be worth going back to page ix to take another look. Where are you now on money? Where are you now on happy?

Let's start with money and have a good look at where you are now with your finances. The hard stuff.

Budgets seem to be the hardest work (sorry Sir Elton)

Number phobe is a description I can answer to. Over the years I have learned how not to come out in hives, or cry, the moment a page of figures is put in front of me. But my lack of numeracy has always been painfully evident. At secondary school I was asked to leave the maths "O" level class. Why? Because of my desperate diversion tactics put into action as soon as the teacher started his regular "round the class maths quiz". After putting a rather dramatic halt to one terrifying quiz (I think it was geometry) I was told firmly that I was never, ever, ever to go near the Convent electrics again.

So, with great empathy for those who fear the word budget, let's proceed.

Even the most basic level of financial awareness is remarkably useful when it comes to being in control of your life. Knowing what you owe, own and earn at broad-brush level will be a huge step forward. Fear of the worst is usually worse than knowing the worst, in terms of cold night sweats and fear of Mr Postman and his terrible envelopes. Imagine feeling more in control of that lot. It could possibly start right now.

The first part is called the Magic Number.

This is quite simply the amount you can spend in any month without going more into debt. In my world of rather simplistic economic management, my goals are to:

(a) be kind to myself and others, in the area of money,

(b) not pay as much in interest as I did for the purchase itself (i.e. to pay off the highest credit cards first),

(c) know how much can come out of the hole in the wall each month without going madly overdrawn.

So to the last point. There is a reason why banks have allowed us greater access to our cash, namely the banking income stream known as overdrafts. Oh yes, I know we enjoy the convenience and all. But given the natural ill discipline of us humans, it seems little surprise that in the UK we have (summer 2004) now passed the trillion pound debt mark. I suspect that you and I have contributed to that amount by regularly withdrawing small amounts of cash from that nice machine in the high street, without having a clue about how much we really can afford to spend. Ten pounds here and there. Sometimes thirty – so easy and, if you are like me, a way to gently exceed every planned budget without so much as noticing.

There are two big choices. Debt repayments and workplace insecurity or financial control and multiple income streams. The do-nothing strategy usually gets you the first of those options. Earn more, spend more, need to earn more. And repeat. Sometimes I do feel very angry about the sale of credit, i.e. debt, to us gullibles, on our shopping travels. Gullibles travels?

The consumer tide takes people out without them even noticing – well out of their depth. Or should I say debth?

So – I present to you, a way to budget your monthly salary, right from the off.

How to calculate the Magic Number (how much you really have to spend each month)

On the day that you get paid (this is very important) calculate the following (I have added some sample figures to illustrate).

QUESTION	COMING IN £	GOING OUT £
Monthly salary or other income paid (gross)	2,500	
How much have you earned (net – the amount paid into your bank account)?	1,800	
What are your regular bills (including mortgage)?		350
Groceries		250
Add total regular monthly bills list here		600
Net income amount minus bills	1,800 − 600 = 1,200	
What are your debt repayments (credit and store cards, student loan)?		200

QUESTION	COMING IN £	GOING OUT £
Add debt list here		100
Total debts each month		300
Net amount, minus regular bills, minus total debts	1,200 − 300 = 900	
Now you can see your disposable spending money for the coming month (already half net income)	**900**	
Now divide this amount by the amount of time to your next salary payment. On this example you have £900 to spend on everything bar essential costs over the month. You could simply do the following sum: £900 divided by 3* weeks = £300 per week (but you need to deduct non-essential costs from that £300 figure) (Or you could estimate all costs before you divide by the amount of time to your next salary payment.) Now, follow the next steps		

➡

* or however many weeks to your next monthly payment

QUESTION	COMING IN £	GOING OUT £
What are your average monthly non-essential living costs (entertainment, games, travel, clothes – look at your previous bank statements and credit cards if you don't know)?		400
What do you need to save to make something happen later on (holiday savings, birthday)?		200
Pension or other savings		100
Average likely spend of disposable income per month (stuff you are likely to buy, each month)		700
Disposable income minus average monthly spend	900 − 700 = 200	
Now you can see your magic number – the amount that you can afford to spend in the month without worrying	**£200**	

So. £200. Which isn't a huge amount each month. But at least you know.

Given the pace of consumer debt, it seems you and I consider the risks of overspending money rather like the risks of smoking. Distant and not certain to apply to me anyway. Certainly not enough to stop anything I plan to do this afternoon.

Does knowing you have £200 to spend (rather than some infinite sum, until the machine stops paying out notes) mean you change your behaviour? Of course not. But it might slow down the impulse purchases, might make sure certain bills get paid before they turn critical. All in all, they might deliver a modicum of control. Which is a very good start.

Now, as you grow heady with the joy of knowing how wealthy you really are, can I offer a borrowed business tool, the income and expenditure account. This simply presents a list of your income and expenditure (surprise, surprise), so you can roughly work out if you are making any profit. The usual word is salary, which, for reasons already discussed, may be profitable or unprofitable. Back to figures. Yours. Specifically.

Imagine being able to predict your financial situation in a year's time. To know if you can afford a holiday, or time away from work, with some knowledge rather than prayer behind you? In this section, if you can, there is the chance to scribble some financial basics down. Then transfer that into a basic profit and loss account. Is anyone still there?

Look. Try it, just off the top of your head first. OK, that would mean assembling your financial information. Are we friendly enough to do that yet?

Top ten things to learn about your own money

Are you able to produce an accurate summary of your personal finance at any time? The questions on the next page might help.

EXERCISE

QUESTION	YOUR UNRESEARCHED ANSWER (OFF THE TOP OF YOUR HEAD)	THE FACTS (MAY TAKE A LITTLE LONGER)
1. What is your current net income per month? Work Other income (dividends, rents)		
2. What is the current value of your investments? (ISAs, shares, assets such as house)		
3. What is the amount of your outstanding *unsecured* debts (credit cards, loans, etc.) minimum to be paid each month?		
4. What is the amount of outstanding *secured* debts (mortgage) to be paid each month?		
5. Total monthly income is . . . Total monthly expenses are . . .		

INCOME/EXPENDITURE PROJECTION	£K 2004 (JAN–DEC)	£K 2005 (JAN–DEC)	£K 2006 (JAN–DEC)
Clothing	2	3	4
Health costs – e.g. eyewear, dental, gym membership	5	6	7
Work-related travel*	2	3	4
Personal tax calculation costs, e.g. accountant*	2	3	4
Charitable donations	2	4	6
IT equipment*	2	2	2
Phone and internet connection (including mobile)*	3	4	5
Stationery and post*	1	0.5	0.5
Insurance*	0.5	0.5	1
Training*	0	2	4
Marketing and PR for products*	1	0.5	1
Total employee expenditure	**15**	**20**	**23**
Income minus expenditure (gross profit)	**15**	**19**	**30**

Two things came out from the discussions involved in getting those figures. First, that the employer takes a lot of costs on board. Second, that disposable income is about half earned income in the first year, without deducting any living costs, bills or credit card payments. So what looks like a good salary translates into very little ready cash. You know that already? OK. That means any increase in personal living costs represents more individual risk – the employer has no duty to pay a larger salary just because mortgage rates increase.

What do you think?

Who bears economic risk?

The current free-market system has evolved to ensure that you and I as individuals cover the economic risk associated with housing, fuel/travel costs, living costs and, increasingly, university education.

OK, no one wants Soviet-style worker dormitories with the state taking on the economic risks of housing and turning life into a miserable sojourn in grey concrete.

However, I do wonder if there might be a free-market design fault, given that those with vital skills (one person who contributed to this exercise is a primary school teacher) are forced to reduce their standard of living because housing is such a high expense. Is it always right for individuals to cover economic risk? What do you think?

To decrease this risk, the employee needs (a) to increase income from other sources (such as assets) and (b) to plan living costs so as not to move into debt. All marvellous in theory, but we all know how difficult it is to work hard and not spend hard.

This exercise in considering income and expenditure projections could be useful if you have plans requiring additional spending in the coming years. For example, you've decided to go to the US for an extended trip next year. The chances are you'll have to create extra income unless you are happy to pay extra for your trip by using a loan or credit cards. The idea of planning increased income does feel strange though – almost like planning better weather for your holiday next year. It's not in your gift. Or is it?

> Your increased income does not solely depend on the workings of the free market, as expressed by your boss. Just as importantly, it depends on how you expand your choices and possibilities.

For example, my ability to choose a low-pay career path is because I have income from assets – specifically rents from investment in residential property. These properties were bought (with my partner) in the last 10 years, during a time when I had higher earnings from salaried employment. The level of rental income is not guaranteed, and has in fact reduced in the past two years when compared with previous years. However, the rental income does cover monthly mortgage payments for all properties and make a small surplus. That surplus pays a good percentage of my living costs. The surplus could be reinvested, for example, to save for further deposits on new property investments, or on renovation work. But right now, my choice is to invest the surplus in time to work on something which feels important and worthwhile – and unpaid (visit www.magicbreakfast.com and www.magicoutcomes.com for more on my day job). If this sounds like a good idea to you,

Some definitions

Professional assets

Specialist knowledge, skill, professional network, experience and capacity to add value to your current workplace. A professional asset makes your employer want to keep you!

Value add

The ability to enhance value of any process, product or service. Being a valued employee means that you know how to add value, which in turn differentiates your product or service from another in the marketplace.

What does your workplace produce. Cars? Ideas? Technology solutions? How do you add value? Useful words here include better performance, better reliability, additional features, lower maintenance cost, higher levels of service.

What value do you add?

The transition from none to some professional assets is perhaps the most important in your career. So, at risk of repeating myself, here is another way to view the process.

FROM PROFESSIONAL ASSETS TO INCOME CREATING ASSETS – THE VIRTUOUS CYCLE

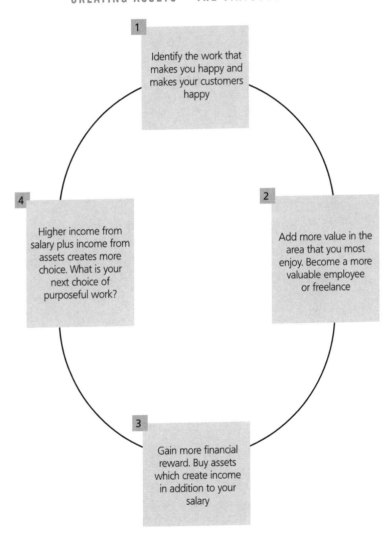

1
Identify the work that makes you happy and makes your customers happy

2
Add more value in the area that you most enjoy. Become a more valuable employee or freelance

3
Gain more financial reward. Buy assets which create income in addition to your salary

4
Higher income from salary plus income from assets creates more choice. What is your next choice of purposeful work?

Smile – your financial snapshot

Below is a template for you to estimate your own income and expenditure snapshot. Even rough estimates will help you see an outline of your options – try it.

INCOME/EXPENDITURE PROJECTION	£K 2004 (JAN–DEC)	£K 2005 (JAN–DEC)	£K 2006 (JAN–DEC)
Income			
Work – usual salary			
Bonus			
Other income (rental income, share dividends)			
Other income 1			
Other income 2			
Asset sales			
Total income			
Expenditure			
Work related costs			
Childcare costs			
Taxi costs			
Other travel and transport costs			

INCOME/EXPENDITURE PROJECTION	£K 2004 (JAN–DEC)	£K 2005 (JAN–DEC)	£K 2006 (JAN–DEC)
Clothing and personal care			
Health costs (eyes, teeth, other medical)			
Study and learning			
Miscellaneous others			
Other costs 1			
Other costs 2			
Other costs 3			
Bills			
electricity,			
water			
heating			
phone			
mobile phone			
cable			
minimum credit card payments			
student loan			
other consumer loan repayments			
Other bills 1			
Other bills 2			
Other bills 3			

To get you thinking about your own definition of happiness, here and at the end of each point are a few questions.

Question 1

Does your life have a strong enough "why" – to help you get through the "how"? In other words, do you have a big challenge or sense of purpose in your life right now?

If yes, what is that "why"?

What kind of "how" does it help you get through?

2 Happiness is not coming second

I'd like to tell you about William James. He was a famous nineteenth century American psychologist who understood the psychological principle of the pain of the near miss, described as follows:

 So we have the paradox of a man shamed to death because he is only the second pugilist or the second oarsman in the world. That he is able to beat the whole population of the globe minus one is nothing; he has pitted himself to beat that one and as long as he doesn't do that nothing else counts.

William James, 1892, *Psychology*

According to this school of thought, you and I will be more unhappy missing a train by five minutes than by 35 minutes. This is known as 'counterfactual thinking' by psychologists, and by that they mean pain caused by dwelling on what might have been. Why does five minutes late for a train cause more upset than 20 minutes? Because you could have made it. Supporting this "so near and yet so far" theory, a famous piece of research conducted by psychologists at Cornell University during the 1992 Summer Olympics at Barcelona, found that silver medalists were more unhappy than bronze medalists. The silver medalist is pained by the belief that he or she almost won the gold medal, whereas the bronze medalist tended to compare himself more with fourth place. Smugly. So the second thing you may not have known about happiness is that it may at times depend on our ability to resist thoughts of what might have been, to not be adversely affected by nearly winning, or nearly being perfect.

Question 2

Do you feel you must always win?

Would you feel hurt by a peer getting promotion over you?

Who are you trying to beat right now, and what might it be doing to you?

3 Happiness comes from simple, everyday things

Ready for some data? OK. This from Cornell University, in an exercise quoted in Raj Persaud's fact-packed book *Staying Sane*. This time researchers worked on a comparison study consisting of 22 major lottery winners, 22 normal people within a control group and 29 paralysed accident victims. Rating themselves on a 6-point scale of happiness ranging from 0 for not at all to 5 for very much, lottery winners, controls (i.e. the non-lottery or accident victims) and quadriplegics were surprisingly close in their ratings of the presence of happiness. Lottery winners at 4, the controls at 3.82 and the quadriplegics at 2.96. As Persaud says "They were not significantly different in how happy they rated themselves likely to be in the future although the quadriplegics scored slightly higher". After a time the quadriplegics became almost as satisfied as the general population, though never quite as much.

The researchers suggest that these findings can be explained by actual happiness being largely determined by the pleasure that you or I take from mundane, everyday events. The problem with winning the lottery (a strange problem) is the upward revision of expectations. Life should now be at the very least, perfect. You've won the lottery! Ordinary life can never again provide the same levels of pleasure as before the big win. This study suggests that, as aspirations rise, our ability to gain pleasure from the same set of circumstances is reduced or to quote the study, "Standards of comparison adjust and follow the perception of reality". Bother.

Question 3
What simple pleasures give you the most happiness?

When and where are you most relaxed and happy?

What do you do to create those simple pleasures on a regular basis?

4 Happiness comes and goes in our lives

I mentioned natural laws earlier on. Money flows and ebbs, and the same with happiness at different times in our lives. Our experiences of happiness and unhappiness alternate and largely balance each other. Psychologists suggest that we can expect that happy and unhappy periods will alternate through our lives and that, generally speaking in the world there are an equal number of happy and unhappy people. In psychology this implication is known as the "zero sum theory" (and no, this is not the same as no maths homework, the definition of happiness for me aged 10–16). And that's the fourth thing you may not have known about happiness.

Question 4

In relation to the ups and downs in your life so far, where are you now? In a less or more happy period? Why do you feel that?

Are you OK with the fact that happiness comes and goes for everyone or do you secretly expect happiness to arrive someday and stay?

5 Happiness is a met need

According to Austrian psychologist Sigmund Freud, unhappiness is caused by unmet needs, such as the need to be free to do what we want, regardless of social rules. So it therefore follows that happiness results from the meeting of those needs. Identify a need, meet it, get happy. By S. Freud. Thank you for number five.

Question 5

What are your top three personal needs, right now?

and make better decisions – their internal rules say – "don't worry, next time you'll do better". Rather than "that's the last time I ever say things out loud during the department's finance meeting".

Question 9

What inner rules are you aware of? For example, "I have to be 100% at everything, or else I'm a loser."

Are they likely to help you create happiness, or not?

How?

10 How we define happiness changes according to the needs of the society around us

The writings of Homer (roughly 900 BC to 700 BC) spoke of valiant heroes such as Odysseus and Achilles. Attributes such as physical strength, courage and endurance were seen as paramount. Gods were mighty and powerful, humanity looked to athletics and the battlefield. During a time of war and insecurity, happiness came from strength and a sense of being victorious. This definition was appropriate for a warrior society.

A different definition had held sway during the earlier period (Imperial Athens 520 BC). During this period virtue, restraint and civic responsibility were key themes, more in keeping with post-war, stable economies with the certainty of colonies and overseas capital. At least until the war with Sparta. Happiness during that age came from being an active citizen, playing a role linked to more social cohesion. Changes in these two periods suggests that definitions of happiness change with our social context. This more settled "middle period" of ancient Greece encouraged growth in intellectual, rather than physical prowess. And with this came Plato's view of happiness drawn from what he described as "the perfection of the soul". In Plato's drama *The Apology* the key speech by Socrates states that life exists to seek wisdom, to encourage the view that it is not wealth and success that make goodness, but that goodness gives value to wealth and success. A controversial view then, as now.

> Plato's student, Aristotle, suggests that happiness is active well-being, and well-doing, or eudaimonia, which means a flourishing state of soul.

Plato argues that goodness follows from a knowledge of the intrinsic value of who we are, and the things we desire.

For persons he described as being "of low tastes" which Aristotle felt to be the majority, he held that the greatest good is pleasure. For the businessman it is wealth and the gentleman believes it is honour. All these are mere instruments to deliver happiness, which is the desired state, sought by all men, in his view.

I wonder what definition of happiness seems most prevalent today. Looking around in 2004, I feel our society has parallels with the Hellenistic period of ancient Greece. Then, as now, we elect warrior leaders, and our heroes come from sport (for example, footballers) more often than from literature. We keenly buy consumer goods such as 4 × 4 vehicles, which aim to represent power and strength. We have a highly militarized economy, where our leaders prioritize national security. Many of these seem to be recycled Hellenistic values, where happiness is about security, being in control and less about openness, tolerance and the pursuit of artistic beauty. Societies may evolve, but there are cycles of war and peace, growth and recession. So perhaps we are due a new age of enlightenment. Anytime soon is good with me!

Question 10

Who are your heroes and heroines and what does that tell you about yourself?

What would be an accurate definition of happiness for you at this moment?

Summary

Section 3 aimed to help you consider where you are now. Where in terms of actual money. Where in terms of your career and material assets. And, in the last few pages, a chance to reflect on your personal approach to finding happiness.

The next section is about moving forward, using three steps. So if you're ready...

How to Make Money, Be Happy?
The three-step approach

> The trouble with fulfilling your ambitions is that you think you are going to be transformed into some sort of archangel and you're not. You still have to wash your socks. Louis de Bernieres, 1999

"Happiness is not a state to arrive at, but a manner of travelling. Margaret Lee Runbeck

04

> Happiness is when what you think,
> what you say, and what you do are in harmony.
> Mahatma Gandhi

What's going on in your head – what are your beliefs?

What do I mean by beliefs? I mean your autopilot in life, the conditioning that means you know which behaviour to use at work, your views, your innermost values.

What you think about turns into the realities in your life – so, for example, if you strongly believe you will always be on the breadline, you'll only apply for low-paid jobs, where you feel you belong. You will choose friends in the same situation. Your thoughts will cause you to limit your beliefs further – in a self-perpetuating cycle of thoughts and behaviours. You may think that money problems are a natural part of life – which means that even if you do earn some extra money, you'll have to get rid of it to be back to normal – no money. Lottery winners are a classic example of this. Ten Ferraris later the multi-millionaire has to wonder why there isn't any money left. It is because of the thoughts that say "no money is normal for me"? In just the same way, rich-list folk believe that creating wealth is normal.

One friend of mine, threatened with a lawsuit for £2m just said "Oh sod it, if we lost £2m we'd be able to make it again anyway". I admire that! Your thoughts may suggest that you don't have the right kind of character, or are too old, or young, or whatever. The fact is, people from every inappropriate background have found a way to make money and be happy.

> **"** Your circumstances are very rarely a credible obstacle to your prosperity.

Actor Jim Carrey had certain beliefs about his future, as demonstrated by this story. In 1990 he worked as a jobbing actor and comedian, not making much progress with his career in Hollywood. In that situation, he wrote himself a cheque for $10m, post-dated to 1995 which read "To Jim Carrey, for acting services rendered, ten million dollars". He has earned $20m for all his films since *The Truman Show*. Even for duds like *Batman Forever*. But I digress from the main point, which is this. Jim Carrey believed in himself and his financial future. This chapter is going to consider the kind of beliefs you hold about yourself, your money and your happiness.

Have you ever written yourself a cheque to be cashed at some future date? If you were to think about it now, what sum would it be for, and for what kind of service rendered? And what date would be on it?

Do your thoughts tell you that people like you don't make money, or become happy? Others do. Do you believe that "no one gets rich unless they start rich?" or "this'll do until I work out something better"? Well fine. The danger is that your compromise becomes your career. And something soul-like can die in a frozen career spot far from the sun of what really matters to you. I am not talking about inevitable happy endings once you get to the top, or into the coolest industries. Believe me, the most envied, cool and well paid career can still be a frozen waste if it ain't right for you. Ask Brad Pitt who just got a job as an apprentice architect so he can design Hollywood 2050; better than a post-idol life of DIY on the Bev Hills palace. Or ask the

Duchess of Kent who, despite a pretty good family network(!) wanted to teach music in a primary school and lived in a rented flat – not the usual monarchical standard.

Do you believe you can just get out, quit the rat race? US comic Lily Tomlin famously said, "even if you win the rat race, you're still a rat". But who wants to quit when others see quitting as personal defeat? "I can't just leave, not after all I've put into it." Well, that's what I thought anyway. A bit like not wanting to walk after 10 minutes at the bus stop. In my case the bus (a little respect in my work) was always about to arrive, just never did. But enough of my career in Information Technology.

How about you? What do you believe?

A beliefs checklist

Tick in the true or false column, next to the answer that most fits your view.

EXERCISE

BELIEFS	TRUE	FALSE
1. I expect my dreams to come true		
2. I am pretty happy about myself, just as I am		
3. I genuinely want success for others as well as myself		
4. There is lots of money available in the world		

BELIEFS	TRUE	FALSE
5. I talk about prosperity and well-being more than debt and problems		
6. My choices expand every day		
7. The answers to my big questions exist within me		
8. I believe things work out for the best		
9. I deserve a life full of money and happiness		
10. I expect the best in people, and am rarely disappointed		
11. I know that my past was full of me doing the best I could at the time. I let go of any earlier mistakes		
12. My goal is to contribute love into the world each day		
13. Everything I do increases my sense of self-worth and value		
14. My debts signify my confidence in future earnings		

→

meaningful challenge, creativity, laughter, energy, purpose, passion, contribution, ideas, health, fun. That kind of thing. The key is to identify the right amount for you.

What is "the right amount" of money? This. You choose a state of financial comfort that is right for you, right now. Your very intimate definition. Not anyone else's. The right amount of security, funds, material comfort, financial recognition, prosperity, cashflow and financial confidence. The value of money largely depends on the value you give it. For some people, their conditioning equates success with money. For others, money is a means to an end. This is not to prescribe your right level, simply to ask you to identify the right amount for you.

What are your beliefs about money?

How happy are you with large amounts of cash? For example, you acquire a very large amount of money. Say £250,000. Imagine your bank account number with £250,000 shown as the latest balance. It is totally legit, and you are able to choose what to do with it.

What is your instant reaction?

- No way could that ever accidentally get into my possession, legally.
- Wonderful, I can do a lot of good in the world with that amount.
- Bloody hell how can I divide it fairly between the family and friends without an almighty bust up?
- Good grief. Now I can take the other half and see the whole wide world.
- Quick, hide it. Or else the taxman will want a piece.
- Great, I can pay off my debts and do something else for a living.
- Hurrah, drinks all round, Caribbean here I come!

As I mentioned, what you think indicates how you are likely to behave. If you think that money is dirty, what kind of behaviour will ensue if you get some? Behaviour to assuage those feelings, or retreat into denial?

In my experience, money beliefs have a direct relation to our confidence and sense of self-worth. This is particularly apparent when it comes to our work.

Many of us hide inside the generic wraparound of being an employee, for example, because our self-worth doesn't permit a direct pitch for a sum of money, based on our market rate. It is much easier to find a job in our desired income bracket, present well at interview and let the nice employer work out the salary details. Anyway, who knows how much anyone is worth per day? Well, the same system works as in any part of capitalism. You are worth what the market will bear in the same way as a property is worth what the buyer is prepared to pay. A big five consulting firm can charge £2k per day for a project manager because the client is prepared to pay. Not necessarily because any pricing of value add and market worth has taken place. Factors such as urgency of skills, client relationship and the firm's brand kudos all add up to a figure the client is prepared to pay. The client believes that £2k per day is a good price to pay. Also, it isn't his or her personal money!

Common beliefs among the seven richest people I know

During this year I met and interviewed seven people who have high personal net worth – enough not to need to work. They all come from a variety of backgrounds and economic starting places.

Their views had some compelling similarities.

1 They had all made a conscious decision to be prosperous.

2 They see their success as directly linked to the quality of their human relationships – with their family, with clients, with their employees.

3 They focus on getting feedback to improve at their work, which has in turn created better products and services. (In a commercial setting this turns into revenue, in a not-for-profit organization it turns into great service quality, happy users and serious promotion).

4 They believe they are responsible for what happens in their life – none of them had a "others are to blame" attitude.

5 They found something they love to do, and which had a strong marketplace appeal and put a lot of effort into it.

6 They are focused on specific results – they all have goals which are very meaningful to them (ranging from grow the firm to this size to buy x kinds of new property).

7 They have all converted surplus income into income producing assets. Those assets reflect their personalities – from holiday homes to media shares to classic cars.

8 They understand how to make money, but spend little intellectual energy focused on it during the day. They are more interested in being creative and doing a great job.

9 They know how to protect their wealth, e.g. they hire good money advisors.

10 They give a lot of money away – nearly all of them are generous hosts and employers (bar one!).

11 They live in the present moment and don't worry about earlier mistakes or future problems "if it's not going to kill you, don't worry about it".

What do you make of that?

Imagine multiple streams of income

Being an employee creates certain beliefs. The focus needed to succeed in one specialist area can create a gulf between what you do now and other career options, until after a few years it feels less possible to move. You and I begin to feel uniquely suited to just one job, i.e. the one we've done for a while. This is a two-way street – employers rarely encourage employees to try other employment avenues – unless they are keen to be seen as progressive or wishing to reduce cost by that awful phrase "headcount reductions". Most employers are keen to retain good employees. Even if your appraisal focuses on things you could have done better, rather than saying thank you and do, please, stay another year.

The net effect of many full-time jobs is a sort of tunnel vision – it becomes harder to see how current skills and expertise could translate into a variety of new and potentially better settings. So, even though many exist, you may not be able to see, or have the confidence to investigate alternative options for your skills or alternative forms of income. You may also feel somewhat dependent on your employer – they do after all have a monopoly position on your labour. And with every monopoly, there is a push to down costs and up production. You may have noticed this, where you work. Also – like any supplier to a monopoly – you do feel somewhat grateful deep down for their continued custom. After all, you do have costs.

So how can you investigate options for more income, or even more varied employment, without risking the whole set up?

Remember Ginger Rogers did everything Fred Astaire did, but she did it backwards and in high heels. Faith Whittlesey

Can you do something more challenging in return for more reward? Or are you not feeling up to it just now?

Consultants, freelancers and contractors already know the ropes on this one. Have a variety of marketable skills and areas of expertise, and offer the most valuable and enjoyable one to the most profitable and secure-looking employer.

There is something to be learned from that approach – which is why I want to offer an example from the freelance world.

Example. How to create multiple income streams

You work as an illustrator for a children's book publishing company. You love the work, but it is on a project basis – contract by contract. So it sometimes feels like you have little security (although, in fact, you were employed 9 out of every 12 months for the past three years). You have debts and regular mortgage payments which need a regular stream of income. The question is, therefore, how to create and retain additional streams of income to tide over the months of no work. This is basically a learning process to decide on one of the many options open to you as a talented person.

Can you:

1 Expand distribution of your skills to a wider audience (same work, more customers). For example, could you search for new customers, illustrate websites or online brochures?

2 Charge more for what you do with some customers (same work, higher value)? Do you know the value of your work to the customer, do you know the cost of equivalent competitors? Do you know your customers' highest priority projects or why they choose you over others? Answer these and perhaps you will be able to negotiate a higher rate of pay.

3 Do something which uses those talents in another, related sphere (same work, different setting)?

4 Do something different for existing customers to bring in cash – where you have a great relationship with the publisher, could you broaden your skills to be able to take on jacket designs or text designs, for example (different work, same setting)?

5 Do something different for new customers – anything from work in a graphics store to being the portrait artist at parties (different work, different settings)?

6 Teach, consult, advise those who want to be where you are (different work, different setting)?

The same thinking process can apply just as well if you are on the payroll as a permanent employee. Imagine you are still an illustrator as before, but you don't want to work full-time for this company any more. You desperately want more freedom. So while you have security (at least, for the moment) the question is how can you carry on doing what you love, as a freelancer, or part-time? Think of your company as a customer and re-read the six options. The same thinking process applies equally well. In both situations you need to shift your beliefs about your employer/customers and create this wider view of income possibilities.

The multiple income stream has to start somewhere. So why not now? Against each one of those, just jot down whatever comes to mind. And see where it takes you.

Exercise. Options for multiple income

Where possible, start by considering the work that makes you happy – and build from there.

■ My earnings would then be . . .

3 Could you do something which uses those talents in another, related sphere (same work, different setting)?

■ What other industries or workplaces intrigue me? Could I do what I do here in another location? . . .

■ Which ones and why? . . .

■ How would I (theoretically, of course) contact them? . . .

■ My earnings from that additional stream would be . . .

4 Could you do something different for your existing employer to bring in more cash (different work, same setting)?

■ What resource shortages exist here (which I could cover)? . . .

■ What would be fun to learn or experience? How could I use it to my career advantage here (more customer experience, more time in the factory or more time on client sites perhaps. Even in a less sexy role!)? . . .

■ Would I want to offer extra hours in exchange for extra pay? In what conditions? . . .

- My earnings from that additional stream would be . . .

5 Could you do something different for a new employer or employers (different work, different settings)?
- What do I love doing outside this job? Is there a way this could become a career option? . . .

- What could I do that is really different (for more on this see *Careers Un-ltd* by myself and Jonathan Robinson, *The Work You Were Born to Do* by Nick Williams)? . . .

- What would I love to do in another location (OK – this becomes alternative not additional income stream, unless you're Dolly the Sheep turned cloned employee!)? . . .

- My earnings from that additional stream would be . . .

6 Teach, consult, advise those who want to be where you are (different work, different setting).
- What knowledge, skill or experience could I pass on to others? . . .

- What are the options for being paid to do that? . . .

- My earnings from that additional stream would be . . .

Ten suggestions to earn more – freelance or contractor view

1 Price right – based on three or four days per week earning time.

2 Work out how much you want to do for your customers for free and keep to it.

3 Share information and build a network for others' success.

4 Recognize that you will underestimate, and build slack into the proposal.

5 Share resources (back office, secretarial) to save costs.

6 Have a passion that means you have a niche specialism.

7 Aim to become a trusted adviser, not an expert.

8 Learn and learn and learn about best practice.

9 Aim for 60% utilization. Let me explain that. You decide you have three days available for freelance or consulting work which can be charged to a client. If you work one of those three days you will be 33% utilized. If you can charge your client for all three of those days you will be 100% utilized. Aim for 60% utilization.

10 Give your advice, experience and money away as much as you possibly can.

Better thoughts

Hopefully you'll have some better insight into your personal beliefs on money. The question is, how to improve those beliefs to *Make Money, Be Happy*.

First of all a little theory. Most psychologists agree that our behaviour is greatly influenced by our dominant thoughts. If those thoughts dwell on fears of insufficient money or being cheated, then more defensive and security-based behaviour is likely to develop. It appears that thoughts about money point to just two basic sets of beliefs.

First is a set of thoughts which say "it's me against the world". This is a fear-based belief, one that says life is going to be full of hard times and scarcity. This will be your mindset if you find yourself thinking the following thoughts.

- Others always seem to have more money than me.
- I'll always be on low pay, because of what I do.
- I've very little choice about how much money I've got.
- I do deserve more money, but life is unfair.
- Money is hard to get and harder to keep.
- I've no idea how people make money.
- I don't know what I want to do with my life.
- I'm always broke, whatever I earn.
- I have to watch out, because others want to get one over on me.
- It's best not to trust others or help them get ahead, because they wouldn't do the same for me.

Does that sound like you? Maybe not – in which case the second approach might be more appropriate. The second approach is "I feel supported by the world", which is an abundance-based belief in good times and plenty. It is a way of thinking where everything is likely to go well, and you are safe from harm. This will be the mindset you inhabit if you think along the following lines.

- I deserve to be well paid.
- I'll find the right income to allow me to live my purpose.

- Life offers lots of wonderful chances to make money.
- Money appears just when I need it.
- I am usually in the right place at the right time.
- I am a prosperous person.
- My dreams come true.
- Making money comes easily to me.
- I use my skills to create wealth for myself and others.
- I am happy to share my good fortune because there is lots of everything to go round.
- I want others to be financially successful.
- I allow and accept prosperity in my life.

Was that more like you? Go back and review the thoughts that you noted down. Gut feel, do they come across as open and prosperous, or closed and hard-done-by? Clearly one of these creates an easier mindset for living a successful life!

> What is your money mindset? One that tells you there's plenty about? Or one that says go out and fight for every scarce quid?

Ten little known things about money

1 The average UK graduate leaves after the first degree with a debt of £13,000.

2 Out of the 2004 *Sunday Times* rich list (showing the 300 wealthiest individuals in the UK) only 11% of the very wealthy had decided to retire.

3 In the UK, 9.3% of GDP (gross domestic product) was spent on pensioner income during 2003. That has to increase to

13% during the next 20 years if living standards for the elderly keep up with the rest of the population (Government Actuaries Report).

4 The *Sunday Times* rich list (2004) shows 751 of the richest 1000 entries are self-made millionaires, and 249 inherited their wealth.

5 Average earnings of full-time male employees were £525 per week in April 2003, for women the average was £396 while the figure for all adults was £476 (Source: Office of National Statistics).

6 There are 12,000 investment clubs in the UK. These are small groups of novice investors, who pool cash and research into shared investments. The largest study on investment club performance (a 10-year study by the National Association of Investors Corporation in the UK) found that all-female clubs turned in annual returns of 24% versus 19% from male clubs. These results are also replicated in the UK – even in falling markets (*Financial Times*, October 03).

7 A survey sponsored by Skandia insurance in the UK (March 2004) found that £5000 is the amount individuals report as being needed to pay off all their debts, apart from the mortgage.

8 Star signs of Britain's richest 1000 (where known) Gemini 110, Taurus 104, Aries 95, Capricorn 92, Aquarius 91, Virgo 88, Libra 87, Leo 84, Sagittarius 84, Cancer 80, Scorpio 79, Pisces 73.

9 In the UK, individual bankruptcies are at their highest level since 1993, official figures have shown. The Department of Trade and Industry (DTI) said there were 10,294 individual insolvencies in England and Wales between January and March 2003.

10 Of those bankruptcies, 899 individuals were full-time students.

Beliefs about happiness – do you have happiness in mind?

> There is no duty we so underrate as the duty of being happy. Robert Louis Stevenson, 1881

I don't know about you, but I have never actively planned happiness. Up until recently, I've vaguely hoped to be happy as a by-product of enjoyable activities, time with loving friends and family. It was bound to happen somewhere along the line.

However, once I realized that happiness could be actively sought, created and spread, my world changed. The same principle of a sequence of beliefs, behaviour and action applies here. We tend to move our lives in the direction of our dominant thoughts. That's where self-fulfilling prophecy comes in. Comes in, sits down and asks for all your biscuits.

Have you ever met someone who said his only desire was to avoid, say, a job which meant sorting out everyone else's problems. Then cheerfully goes off into job number three with "unpaid counsellor" written all over it. Or someone who said "I will never work in a bank like my father, never", then goes into financial services for five years. Why do you think that happens? According to every psychologist and NLP expert it is because, let me say it again, we move in the direction of our dominant thoughts, even when those thoughts point to something we so don't want to do. "Careful you don't fall over running down that road" will cause the child to do just that. Thanks mum. "I must not leave the car keys on the kitchen table" will also cause you to do just that. Which is why all the good NLP people would train you to think "I will put my car keys in my jacket pocket now while I remember". No amount of NLP can remind you which jacket, however. You only remember the right one, and its location in your wardrobe, while standing next to the car 10 minutes away, down the road.

So if you think "I refuse to work for a workaholic boss in my next job" what does your brain hang onto? Workaholic boss. Next time. Got it. Then, well here you go again. Or if you think "I can never find the right answers with customer queries, no wonder they get angry" what behaviour does that invite? In just the same way, if you think about the ideal circumstances for your next job, the beautiful location, the supportive boss – whatever – it is more likely to happen. I know it sounds a bit Disney, but happiness begets happiness. The more you have an internal portfolio of happy achievements, the more you are likely to attract more of the same. So, as a practice run, when was the last time you thought of something and got it, and it made you happy? Run that memory through again – that recollection might well enable you to come up with better ideas about your next ambition. It is not only lovely to think about what makes you happy, evidence suggests that happiness begets happiness. What do you enjoy? What is going well in your life right now? Who do you love? Did you see the evening sky move from gold to red tonight?

If you now buy the idea that your behaviour moves in the direction of your dominant thoughts, what career path is being concocted by your thinking here and now, today? Your career path will move in the direction of your dominant thoughts. I know this is being repeated. I just think that the concept is revolutionary.

The difficulty with dominant thoughts is that they lie dormant, unknown virtually, until we behave in a certain way that indicates our true views. Who knows what party you really support until voting day? Or what you really think about Stuart in marketing until his leaving do. "Sorry, got my ironing planned that night."

Let me try an analogy. The route and destination of your local bus is displayed on the front of the bus. In my case, the 134 goes from Muswell Hill to Tottenham Court Road station in central London. The route of your career is written in big easy-to-read thoughts on the inside of your head. Stop long enough to notice your dominant thoughts and you'll also be able to notice your autopilot career direction. So you have two choices. Career-wise, get on anything that starts moving, then repeatedly throw yourself off when it goes somewhere you'd rather not be. Or read the thoughts, even steer the thoughts, and enjoy the ride to someplace you would actively choose to go. What would you prefer? OK. I know that inner beliefs take some work to read, and moving a career forward isn't as easy as getting on a bus. But it is do-able. Let me show you.

First of all, some questions about your happiness. Yes, I know I started asking these earlier on – I wanted to get you warmed up for this.

When do you feel truly happy? What are you doing? Where and when do you feel – this is me? Nothing could be better. What do you think as you finish work on the last day before a summer holiday? Or when family all make it over for dinner on Friday night. Or when you've got the flat to yourself and can play music, have a long soak in the bath in peace. Or when your children give you a big hug and a kiss for no reason other than they love you. Or when your exams are over and it's a sunny day. What do you think then? Well, fine if you say I think nothing, because it is a feeling. Yes, happiness is a feeling. It is chemical reaction to positive stimuli. My challenge is to ask you to figure out what thoughts accompany those feelings. To be specific. There is more on your beliefs on page 124, this is to get you to discover what is happening at the moment.

As with the money exercise, I ask that you keep a page in your notebook with a header "happiness thoughts". Note these happiness-related thoughts down, as and when you become aware of them. At first it may feel hard – once again don't judge or censor them, just note them down.

Keep going for a week or so. Over this period of time a pattern will emerge – the most common thoughts are likely to be your deep-rooted beliefs about happiness.

Some example thoughts on happiness can be spotted by the force of their opposite theme. "Hope I don't bump into Susan, because she always brings me down" just before Susan is spotted in your favourite coffee shop, enjoying a small life crisis and a blueberry muffin. Or if you notice yourself thinking on the plane "I never relax on holiday, something always goes wrong back home" you'll most certainly enjoy two weeks worth of sun, sand, sea and stress. Alternatively how about "I really want to work on that project, because the people are great and it will make me happy to do something that I find challenging". Or "I really enjoy weekends away on my own, walking the coast. When shall I book the next one?". There is a huge cringe factor in becoming aware of happy thoughts. They're culturally unwelcome in the UK anyway. "Wow mum, those clothes you've bought me are great. I'm so happy" is more likely to come out as "cheers mum, how much do I owe you?" I urge you to get over the cringe factor and figure out what thoughts accompany the moments when you are simply relaxed, happy, chilled, enjoying yourself. Not easy, no. But do it for a week or so, and by that time you will start to notice a pattern – some thoughts repeating themselves and merging into key themes. Generally, patterns in your thinking about happiness point to two basic sets of beliefs. Yes I know that is just the same as money. It is the same!

Let's look at some typical thought patterns. First is a set of thoughts which say "it's me against the world", which is a fear-based belief in hard times and scarcity. This will be the mindset you inhabit if you often think along the following lines.

AN EXAMPLE OF ONE OF YOUR REGULAR THOUGHTS	LIKELY BEHAVIOUR RESULT
I never know my career direction. Lets just see how it goes	■ Less commitment to current role as not sure of future plans ■ Feel inadequate and low in confidence believing others have a great plan ■ Fear for the future – no sense of the options ■ Sense of drift – perhaps made up for with short-term highs such as shopping or trips away
No one will ever notice all the work I do round here	■ Feeling of resentment, of being used ■ Low self-worth ■ Anger at others – perhaps not expressed outwardly ■ Exhaustion from feeling put upon

THE OPPOSITE	LIKELY BEHAVIOUR RESULT
I know my career direction. What I do today is part of what I want to learn about longer term	■ Start listening at meetings ■ Real interest in current role as important part of future plans ■ Feel confident and able to relate well to peers – feeling of common purpose ■ Optimism about the future – may not have the details worked out, but strong sense of the options
People really value the work I do here	■ Sense of belonging – feel included rather than excluded ■ Sense of being valued and respected ■ High self-worth ■ Warm connection with others – leading to trust and good communication ■ Energy from work that feels recognized and valued

Now try it with something that springs to mind – literally – for you, just now. I know it seems a bit strange to just switch it round. It does make a difference though – simply because your brain takes instructions from the program of your thinking in exactly the same way as your laptop performs according to the software loaded onto it.

Your thoughts are the program. Your life is what is on display from the program running behind.

One of my most dominant thoughts right now would be …

This could lead me to behave like this …

The opposite thought would be …

And the opposite behaviour would be …

Happiness is a largely self-directed state, unless you want to remain at the mercy of the world forever. There comes a time in your life when you work out whether being happy is yours to control, or the gift of someone else.

When happiness is a state you can choose to change, rather than blame the various disempowering "they" in your life, you can begin to gain real control. What do I mean by "they"? They might be, for example, the boss who won't let you do the work you really want to do. Or the kids who have school fees that force daddy to stay in a job he hates, but which pays well. "They" could be the parents who say they really want to be proud of you and, you do know there has always been a doctor in the family?

If you wait for happiness to arrive courtesy of the "they" chances are you'll be waiting a long time – simply because you cannot control what other people choose to think. Psychologists offer the view that self-belief about how much happiness you can have is the singlemost influential factor in determining how happy you actually are. Reason enough to decide to be happy sooner rather than later?

What makes me happy?

"One of the things that I've noticed is that those people who just go after money are very worried about spending anything. And if you want to make money you have got to be a bit of a gambler. The other thing is, I don't think about money. When I am doing up someone's home, I think about how nice I can make a place, the colours, how I can bring it all together so it can be a place of cheer and rest for the people that stay here. So I don't think to myself 'Oh, if I do this, I'm going to get this.' I think 'what kind of curtains will look really nice in this room?' Creating a place of cheer and comfort is what I really enjoy."

Sheila J. (creates lovely holiday homes in West Cornwall)

Behaviours

I have, all my life long, been lying until noon; yet I tell all young men, and tell them with great sincerity, that no one who does not rise early will ever do any good. Samuel Johnson, 1785

The second part of the journey to *Make Money, Be Happy* is based around behaviours. As we have discussed, your beliefs about money and happiness are likely to manifest in how you behave in these areas. Here we will look at some behaviours which you may have adopted on autopilot, and also propose some behaviours to ensure you move your story forward. Starting with money behaviours.

How Andy Made Money, Be Happy

Lets take an example. Andy is a recently qualified gym instructor and track athlete who has competed at country level. On the four states grid, Andy is in the top-left hand corner "I make no money, but I am happy". Well, he does make a little money.

His CV shows extra qualifications (e.g. nutrition advisor), but it still took a while to find his current job, as there are not many fitness centres in his town. He makes just enough to cover his rent, student loan and outgoings. He can't save on current earnings and is worried about the future. But he was delighted to be taken on and does believe this is his ideal job.

First question – how's the job going? Great – at first. But six months on, getting tired of being the gym junior, always expected to go-fetch for everyone in the gym team. The thing he thought he would enjoy most – individual planned sessions – is a job reserved for the senior team members. Andy finds this pecking order frustrating – especially as he cannot see a way to earn more in the next 12 months.

What can Andy do to make more money? Back to the core approach, i.e. purposeful profit; to work out what makes him happy and find people who will pay him to do it. Andy has done the first part already – working on something he really enjoys, and a market for his skills – the local health club.

Now he needs to focus more on that happiness, come up with a clearer view of what he most enjoys about the job. Then find as many ways as possible to make money doing it. How does the advice above become Andy's personal *Make Money, Be Happy* strategy? The following pages work that through in detail. Perhaps you could see where your own *Make Money, Be Happy* story could move forward, at the same time?

After a run through on the advice above, Andy decides he wants to:

1 Remember what he loves most.

2 Become more valuable in the day job.

3 Distribute valuable know-how to a wider paying audience.

4 Maintain and grow credibility in his field (not just field events, no).

5 Try to cut down on unnecessary costs.

Part 1   What makes Andy happy now?

WHAT MAKES ANDY HAPPY AT WORK? HIS TOP TEN	CAN HE CARRY ON DOING THIS?
1. Helping people become fitter and stronger by getting into exercise	Yes
2. Playing sport, e.g. participating in track events	Yes
3. Being asked for his advice on technique	Yes
4. Finishing early on Fridays	No!

WHAT MAKES ANDY HAPPY AT WORK? HIS TOP TEN	CAN HE CARRY ON DOING THIS?
5. Feeling that the gym is buzzing, not boring	Yes
6. Organizing each individual fitness programme, to have a combination of nutrition and exercise	Not right now
7. Coaching young track athletes	Not much
8. Watching the best athletes train, learning from them	Yes
9. A thank you from the senior team – recognition	Not much
10. Getting personally fitter by working out regularly	Yes

Part 2   Can Andy earn more money through the things that make him happy?

Why is he worth paying? Well, the gym charges a monthly membership of £45. There are 100 members. In addition, members pay extra for treatments and personal training. The gym has an income of approximately £14,000 per month, after running costs. Andy is paid just over £1,000 per month, and is one of four full-time employees. (OK, this is a vastly simplified business model!)

Andy is seen as a qualified instructor capable of providing a good basic-level advice and motivation. He is not considered to have sufficient interpersonal skills or experience, to work with individual clients, but may do so in a year or so.

The next pages follow his thought process, as he identifies a way to make more money through the parts of the job he most enjoys.

WHAT MAKES ANDY HAPPY AT WORK? HIS TOP TEN	CAN HE CARRY ON DOING THIS?
1. Helping people become fitter and stronger by getting into exercise	Yes
2. Playing sport, e.g. participating in track events	Yes
3. Being asked for his advice on technique	Yes No! Yes Yes Yes
4. Finishing early on Fridays	
5. Feeling that the gym is buzzing, not boring	

HOW CAN HE MAKE MORE MONEY DOING THIS?	WHICH ONE IS MOST LIKELY?
▨ Through extra work, e.g. overtime	▨ Possibility of overtime – but doesn't want to
▨ By finding out if he can work with clients privately, with gym management permission	▨ Would be keen to coach clients privately, but doesn't think gym will allow it
▨ By offering gym instruction to other places, e.g. training at local schools	▨ Already coaches for free at old secondary school sports events – wouldn't feel right asking for money
▨ Unlikely to earn money through this as not in top league – but could develop as a top-flight coach	▨ Would love to become a top coach, but doesn't know how
▨ Offering existing gym customers top-up advice via phone or email – with gym management permission	▨ Would love to become a top coach, but doesn't know how
▨ Advising sports websites, magazines if the gym allows	▨ Doesn't feel confident or experienced enough to offer advice to magazines or websites.
▨ Contacting broadcasters to find out about becoming a pundit	▨ Does enjoy working on the gym newsletter and could do more
	▨ Doesn't fancy punditry
Er. No	Would love to do more of this …
Can't see a way right now at this gym	Not likely

➜

WHAT MAKES ANDY HAPPY AT WORK? HIS TOP TEN	CAN HE CARRY ON DOING THIS?
6. Organizing each individual fitness programme, to have a combination of nutrition and exercise	Not right now
7. Coaching young track athletes	Not much
8. Watching the best athletes train, learning from them	
9. A thank you from the senior team – recognition	Not much
10. Getting personally fitter by working out regularly	Yes

HOW CAN HE MAKE MORE MONEY DOING THIS?	WHICH ONE IS MOST LIKELY?
▨ Perhaps adding a nutrition element to existing gym plans – the gym might think this is worth extra pay? ▨ Also offering to work with private clients on their nutrition plans – with permission	▨ Would like to explore this – but unsure how the senior team will react
▨ Is there potential to work with schools and colleges to support practice sessions, sports days? ▨ Do any of the national agencies like Community Sport offer expenses or payment for this?	▨ Loves doing this, doesn't see any money in it
Can't see a way	Not enough access to premier athletes to be a real starter. Where is Kelly Holmes when he needs her?
No	No
No	Will do this anyway, regardless

So Andy has worked out that more money could be made. The question is – how to convince the gym management that he does have the skills to work 1–1. If he does this, doors will open. How to convince the gym senior team? Probably by gaining their confidence slowly, being mentored, letting them know he is keen to offer his help even if it means some extra effort. Gaining the owner's trust in his commitment is key.

Part 3   How Andy could make more money – and wider lessons . . .

The next section shows Andy's priorities, as well as offering ideas on how to *Make Money, Be Happy*, for anyone to use.

WHAT MAKES ANDY HAPPY AT WORK? HIS TOP TEN	HOW CAN HE MAKE MORE MONEY DOING THIS?	WIDER LESSONS FROM THIS APPROACH. COULD YOU USE THESE IDEAS?
1. Helping people become fitter and stronger by getting into exercise	■ Through extra work, e.g. overtime ■ By finding out if he can work with clients privately, with gym management permission ■ By offering gym instruction to other places, e.g. training at local schools	■ Can you add money by adding hours if you have to? (Don't put health second though . . .) ■ Is there an extra audience for your current skills? ■ How could you distribute your expertise to a wider paying audience?

WHAT MAKES ANDY HAPPY AT WORK? HIS TOP TEN	HOW CAN HE MAKE MORE MONEY DOING THIS?	WIDER LESSONS FROM THIS APPROACH. COULD YOU USE THESE IDEAS?
2. Playing sport, e.g. participating in track events	▪ Unlikely to earn money through this as not in top league – but could develop as a top-flight coach over time, with the right sponsors	▪ Is there something that you really enjoy within your job, but which doesn't have a natural money making angle? Keep going – focus on what you love doing and you will be more able to create joy and a sense of aliveness
3. Being asked for his advice on technique	▪ Offering existing gym customers top-up advice via phone, "coachline", or email. Chargeable and only with gym management permission ▪ Perhaps offering advice to sports websites, maga-zines if the gym allows	▪ Can you become a spokesperson for your professional specialism or industry niche? ▪ Do your opinions help others clarify theirs? What are the outlets for this – websites, confer-ences, blogs? ▪ Can you offer advice to the trade publications or

WHAT MAKES ANDY HAPPY AT WORK? HIS TOP TEN	HOW CAN HE MAKE MORE MONEY DOING THIS?	WIDER LESSONS FROM THIS APPROACH. COULD YOU USE THESE IDEAS?
	▓ Offering to add comments at local or national track meetings – getting in touch with the broadcasters to find out the process of becoming a pundit	become a "quote source" for columnists ▓ How can you broker your success story and that of your employer into a wider marketplace?
4. Finishing early on Fridays	▓ Er. No	No. Likely to cause less
5. Feeling that the gym is buzzing, not boring	▓ Can't see a way right now at this gym	▓ What makes your workplace more enjoyable to be in? How can you help create an environment that supports your best performance as well as that of your colleagues? Don't wait for it, offer it
6. Organizing each individual fitness programme, to have a	▓ Perhaps adding a nutrition element to existing gym plans – the gym	▓ Could you offer to support individuals in your workplace, either as a mentor

WHAT MAKES ANDY HAPPY AT WORK? HIS TOP TEN	HOW CAN HE MAKE MORE MONEY DOING THIS?	WIDER LESSONS FROM THIS APPROACH. COULD YOU USE THESE IDEAS?
combination of nutrition and exercise	might think this is worth extra pay? ■ Also offering to work with private clients on their nutrition plans – with permission	or coach or could you develop a way to educate your colleagues in a useful way? And what about the wider audience – could you share across industry or with non-competing firms?
7. Coaching young track athletes	■ Is there potential to work with schools and colleges to support practice sessions, sports days? ■ Do any of the national agencies like Community Sport offer expenses or payment for this?	Probably not much – but free work gains valuable experience and great track record (urrrggg!)
8. Watching the best athletes train, learning from them	■ Can't see a way	■ How can you shadow the role models for your future success?

It is well worth exploring these six options some more:

1 The hard work option

- Can you add money by adding hours if you have to?
- Is there an extra audience for your current skills?
- How could you distribute your expertise to a wider paying audience?

SOME QUESTIONS FOR YOU	GUT FEEL RESPONSES (USE THIS COLUMN TO JOT DOWN SOME THOUGHTS . . .)
1. If you need money, are you prepared to add extra time, e.g. weekend or evening cover?	
2. Is there an extra audience for my current skills?	
3. Who else might be willing to pay you to do what you do – contracting, freelancing or full-time?	
4. What might a nice, easy baby step look like to finding out about the most realistic option?	
Other questions . . .	

Optional actions

1 What could I do?

2 What would the benefits be if I did all or some of them (my accelerators)?

- To me
- My workplace (including customers)
- To my family
- To others

3 What might be stopping me (my brakes)?

4 What is the opposite of each one of those brake statements (just write the opposite and read it again)?

2 The premium option

- Andy thinks "Could I become coach to the top athletes who attract sponsorship. What is the most lucrative way to do what I do?"

HOW DOES THIS APPLY, RIGHT NOW?	WHAT DO I THINK? (USE THIS COLUMN TO JOT DOWN SOME THOUGHTS . . .)
1. Who are the best in your world of work and what do they charge? How did they become able to charge that premium, compared to you? Is it their network, professional specialism, unique talent or deal making ability?	

HOW DOES THIS APPLY, RIGHT NOW?	WHAT DO I THINK? (USE THIS COLUMN TO JOT DOWN SOME THOUGHTS . . .)
2. Of that group, who are your personal role models (people with more experience, that you admire, who are inspiring and impressive in some way)?	
3. What are their goals and issues? Can you contribute something to help? Preferably linking to work that you love.	
4. What could you offer them by way of contribution or do they like "putting something back" by mentoring (you)?	
5. What might a nice, easy baby step look like to making contact with the best?	
Other better questions . . .	

Optional actions

1 What could I do?

2 What would the benefits be if I did all or some of them (my accelerators)?

- To me
- My workplace (including customers)
- To my family
- To others

3 What might be stopping me (my brakes)?

4 What is the opposite of each one of those brake statements (just write the opposite and read it again)?

3 The media option

- Andy thinks "Become an athletics sports pundit, columnist or website contributor."

How might the media option help increase your profile and income. Let's see . . .

HOW DOES THIS APPLY, RIGHT NOW?	WHAT DO I THINK? (USE THIS COLUMN TO JOT DOWN SOME THOUGHTS . . .)
1. What can you do to build more professional credibility in your area? What know-how can you usefully share? Can you write, speak or blog to extend your know-how to a wider audience? How does this help your boss?	
2. Is there a trade magazine or industry website that might want to share your unique insight? What is the win–win for your employer if you do this?	
3. Could you add a column or more regular contribution to either of those?	
4. Does anyone in your sphere speak at conferences? How does that work and have you got a story to tell?	
5. Have you any specialist knowledge that means you could add comment for local or national media? In which situations? And why you?	

HOW DOES THIS APPLY, RIGHT NOW?	WHAT DO I THINK? (USE THIS COLUMN TO JOT DOWN SOME THOUGHTS . . .)
6. How else could you get your message across using newsletters, local events or related articles?	

Optional actions

1 What could I do?

2 What would the benefits be if I do all or some of them (my accelerators)?

- To me
- My workplace (including customers)
- To my family
- To others

3 What might be stopping me (my brakes)?

4 What is the opposite of each one of those brake statements (just write the opposite and read it again)?

4 The consulting option

- Andy thinks "Could I work out what makes the gym enjoyable and help the team do more of it? Could I act like an internal consultant?"

HOW DOES THIS APPLY TO YOU, RIGHT NOW?	WHAT DO I THINK? (USE THIS COLUMN TO JOT DOWN SOME THOUGHTS . . .)
1. If you had a magic wand, what three things would you change to make your workplace a better place to be and why?	
2. Does the customer view get enough airtime in your meetings/processes? Consultants often make their money by representing the customer. Why?	
3. Who would be the best internal sponsor for your "internal consultancy improvements"? Every consultant needs a champion – who is yours?	
4. Is there one way that the firm could simply reduce cost without ruining things? Suggest it and either (a) get a percentage, (b) get a trade in terms of training budget, or (c) get recognition	
5. Would you be OK with rejection of your ideas? Consultants get lots of "no thank you" calls. Will you come back with a better plan or will the first "no" crack your fragile ego?	

Optional actions

1 What could I do?

2 What would the benefits be if I do all or some of them (my accelerators)?

- To me
- My workplace (including customers)
- To my family
- To others

3 What might be stopping me (my brakes)?

4 What is the opposite of each one of those brake statements (just write the opposite and read it again)?

5 The contribution option

- Andy thinks "how could I use my skills to help those who might not be able to afford gym membership? Apart from coaching at my old school, what is the most socially aware way to do what I do?"

HOW DOES THIS APPLY, RIGHT NOW?	WHAT DO I THINK? (USE THIS COLUMN TO JOT DOWN SOME THOUGHTS . . .)
1. What have you got to offer to help someone? How do you feel about reaching out – even out of your comfort zone?	

HOW DOES THIS APPLY, RIGHT NOW?	WHAT DO I THINK? (USE THIS COLUMN TO JOT DOWN SOME THOUGHTS . . .)
2. Why does what you do make a difference in the world? How can you help others understand that?	
3. What will it give you, personally, to know your skills are really making that difference? For example, could you find out if a charity could use your skills? (Hey, what's that www.magicbreakfast.com doing on fitness for inner city primaries these days?)	
4. Who in your family or local area or immediate circle would like some of your help? Can you reach out with your skills close to home?	
5. How can your contribution link into those of other people? What is the combined impact of a group of people like you in the world?	
Other better questions . . .	

Optional actions

1 What could I do?

2 What would the benefits be if I do all or some of them (my accelerators)?

■ To me

■ My workplace (including customers)

■ To my family

■ To others

3 What might be stopping me (my brakes)?

4 What is the opposite of each one of those brake statements (just write the opposite and read it again)?

6 The contract-out option

■ Andy thinks "I know some great athletes who could work at the gym on basic exercise routines, under my instruction. They need extra cash, so do I. OK, maybe this is not for now, but perhaps in a year or so. I could hire them for £10 per hour and charge the gym £12. Maybe I could be a broker, help the gym and the athletes and make some extra money that way? Could I contract out?"

HOW DOES THIS APPLY TO YOU, RIGHT NOW?	WHAT DO I THINK? (USE THIS COLUMN TO JOT DOWN SOME THOUGHTS . . .)
How do you add value, right now? 1. What is the most valuable part of your job to your firm? Why do they pay you?	
2. Does the employer need more of that skill or service than you can provide?	
3. Does it have to be you personally, that provides it?	
4. Do you have the knowledge to price the labour and negotiate that introduction?	
5. Do you have the allies – a network that you could use first to investigate this?	
6. Which other employers might need help this way?	
7. Do you know of other people who would truly benefit from being introduced as providers of this extra labour? Who are your skilled associates?	

Optional actions

1 What could I do?

2 What would the benefits be if I do all or some of them (my accelerators)?

    ▓ To me

    ▓ My workplace (including customers)

    ▓ To my family

    ▓ To others

3 What might be stopping me (my brakes)?

4 What is the opposite of each one of those brake statements (just write the opposite and read it again)?

Out of those six options, maybe one or two jumped out at you. What small action could you take, with the biggest outcome? How could your career appreciate in value? The opposite might help on this.

Depreciation

I know this sounds a little personal, but can I just ask, are you depreciating? And if so, what can you do about it?

Depreciation is defined (rather boringly) as the declining value of a capital asset (such as IT hardware) due to wear and tear and obsolescence. For many people, ideas and specialist expertise are their main personal assets in a knowledge economy.

> ## What you think and do can grow rusty too.

The idea of depreciation therefore is worth translating – the depreciation of your intellectual assets, that is. For example, do you proudly present key points of Total Quality Management (circa 1985) to a peer group that lives and breathes 6 Sigma (circa 2005)? Do you hang onto the last parts of your student rebel self by telling friends work is really boring, subconsciously sabotaging any parts you really enjoy? Cynicism may feel cool at the time, but in my experience the habit shuts down creativity, new relationships, other options.

AM I GETTING RUSTY? A QUIZ

IS YOUR WAY OF THINKING OR WORKING OUT OF DATE?	ANSWERS
1. How are you adapting to blue-tooth and wi-fi technology (this is nothing to do with your spouse, sir)	
2. What is the importance of your company code of governance?	
3. Do you leave your career management to HR?	
4. Do you know how to manage a geographically dispersed team?	

5. At industry level, in your field of work, what are the pros and cons of: – outsourcing non-core processes? – non-hierarchical leadership? – the US economy being overtaken by the Chinese economy? – large-scale national lawsuits against developed world economies by developing world economies, for damages from climate change caused by industrial output?	
6. Do you understand the ideas behind pay per use shared services?	
7. Which competitors are likely to lead your industry in five years time and why?	

Ideas, answers and more resources at www.makemoneybe-happy.com.

THIS IS WHAT I THINK	THIS IS, POTENTIALLY, HOW I'LL BEHAVE	WHAT ARE MY BELIEFS OR BEHAVIOUR IN THIS AREA?
	▨ Become very dissatisfied and turned off by work ▨ Living short term	
Another example of my views about money	The behaviour this might appear as . . .	
Example I'm always broke, whatever I earn	▨ Run up debts, believing that debt is going to happen whatever. Then either have to work longer hours or find other ways to finance the debt ▨ A stressful life, whatever	
A last one from me . . .		
Example I have to watch out, because others want to get one over on me	▨ Staying closed to new friendships, not developing trust amongst work colleagues	

THIS IS WHAT I THINK	THIS IS, POTENTIALLY, HOW I'LL BEHAVE	WHAT ARE MY BELIEFS OR BEHAVIOUR IN THIS AREA?
	▪ Keeping a distance and being seen as a loner or aloof, which becomes a self-fulfilling prophecy	

If you have noticed a particular thread appearing, for example that you don't know what to do next, try this nifty little technique. It feels like cheating alright, but try it anyway.

Where you have written something like "I don't know what to do with my life" simply write the opposite, "I do know what to do with my life". Then let your mind wander on that sentence. Given that your brain works like a computer (I may have mentioned this before) you can open up all sorts of new thoughts by writing the opposite to the one that seems true. Open up new ways to create better options. So if it doesn't look right, over-write it. Just try it?

The link between thought, behaviour and money

What if some of your thoughts were always going to keep you poor and unhappy? Wouldn't it be useful to know about them? In this next section, I have offered some examples of how thoughts and behaviours turn into the norm for how you manage your life. The goal is to get you to think through your own approach.

Questions

1 How do you expect to fund your life (work-related income only, asset-related income only, or a mixture)?

2 What will your net worth be in five, ten and twenty years from now?

3 What is the role of professional advisers during key decisions in your life? Do you take major decisions based on the best available advice (even if it is expensive) or do you take decisions based on personal experience, limited research and your best guess?

4 Do you play an active or passive role when it comes to making money? For example, do you forecast what will happen to your career, the industry or professional context it is in, interest rates or other aspects of your economy. And then take action? Or do you play it as it comes, and believe that those things are largely out of your control?

Taking that idea one step further, the next section considers two ways of funding your life.

What do you choose to live on, assets or income?

A QUESTION	THOSE WITH ASSETS	THOSE WITHOUT ASSETS – JUST INCOME
1. Do I choose to live from month to month on a salary, or do I choose to build assets?	Traditionally, only some people have assets, such as property and shares. These earn money which can be used as income, all the time. Even while their owners are asleep	Other people do not have assets which create income. Their only option is to create income by selling their labour, i.e., from the daily duty of turning up at work. And the rule is no guarantee of work, no guarantee of income.

An example – life with assets:

A richer example

Matthew has a key asset. He owns his own home (the asset in question) and has a housemate. He earns £500 per month rent on the house and pays £600 per month mortgage. Having to meet only £100 per month mortgage costs gives Matthew more flexibility with other income, so he works part-time and studies part-time.

Another example, life without assets:

A poorer example

Ian has no income-generating assets and relies on income. He earns £250 per week in his current job. He rents a flat which costs £130 per week and tries to keep living costs below £110 per week. Unexpected one-off costs often go on credit cards. He is thinking about taking another job such as bar work.

Now over to you.

My current thoughts:

MY BELIEFS ABOUT ASSETS AND INCOME, GENERALLY . . .	WHAT ARE MY BELIEFS ABOUT THOSE WITH ASSETS?	WHAT ARE MY BELIEFS ABOUT THOSE WITHOUT ASSETS?

My current behaviours:

THE AREA OF CORE BELIEF	MY ASSETS	MY WAYS OF GENERATING INCOME, WITHOUT ASSETS
This is how I choose to fund my life. . . .		

How do you take big financial decisions?

THE AREA OF CORE BELIEF	THOSE WITH ASSETS	THOSE WITHOUT ASSETS
How do I take the big decisions in my life? With or without professional advisers?	The most wealthy individuals (who tend to be those with the most assets) have professional advisers who cover most money decisions. These include tax and investment, inheritance, favourable residency and preferential credit terms. Generally, how to manage family finances like a company	Other people do not tend to hire professional advisers, and instead research, learn from peers and generally teach themselves how to take major money decisions. They therefore rely on government agencies for tax advice, the bank for debt management and tend to reside where they can afford housing

An example – taking the big decisions with a professional adviser:

A richer example

The richer Smith family employ an accountant who ensures the main family breadwinner (their mother, an IT contractor) earns income through a limited company rather than as a sole trader. The family saves on tax overall as her earnings are within the higher 40% tax bracket, and the mother saves by claiming work-related expenses.

Another example, without advisers:

A poorer example

The poorer Jones family breadwinners are both full-time employees. They pay higher tax overall as both their earnings are taxed at 40%. They are not able to claim any tax deductions and are not aware of how to minimize their tax bill.

What do you actually do at the moment?

HOW DO I TAKE THE BIG DECISIONS IN MY LIFE?	WHAT DO I FEEL ABOUT USING PROFESSIONAL ADVISERS?	WHAT ARE MY BELIEFS ABOUT TAKING BIG FINANCIAL DECISIONS MYSELF?

What is my current choice?

THE AREA OF CORE BELIEF	MY CURRENT RANGE OF PROFESSIONAL ADVISERS	MY WAYS OF MAKING DECISIONS, WITHOUT PROFESSIONAL ADVISERS
This is how I choose to take major financial decisions		

Do you have a pro-active or passive attitude to your financial life, for example, do you stay informed and seek to forecast what will happen to your career and the industry or professional context it is in? Do you look at what is happening on interest rates, rates of pay or other aspects of your economy, and then take action? Or do you leave it to the experts, play it as it comes, and believe that those things are largely out of your control?

THE AREA OF CORE BELIEF	THOSE WITH ASSETS	THOSE WITHOUT ASSETS
Do I have an active or passive attitude to my financial well-being?	Some people are financially creative and pro-active in terms of the financial environment and how it will affect them. They will, for example, switch their capital investment from risky to less risky portfolios based on market conditions. That could be from buy-to-let property investment to the stock market, depending on market conditions	Other people tend to play catch up, staying pre-occupied with day-to-day life and not looking forward to their financial future. This often means working out too late about interest rates, tax changes and how any job-related financial changes will affect them. They will, for example, find themselves facing rising interest rate mortgages, with a variable rate mortgage, having guessed that interest rates were reasonably stable

An example – a pro-active attitude and approach:

A richer example

The richer Stephen sold his one bedroom buy-to-let flat in central Leeds when his rental return showed a yield of 6% net after maintenance costs. This was because interest rates had increased and increased supply on buy-to-lets had depressed the rental income. Instead he invested in a 6.2% long term investment account, and reduced the hassle of tenants and maintenance.

Another example – this time a reactive approach

A poorer example

The poorer Stuart has been priced out of his one bedroom flat as the neighbourhood has been taken over by buy-to-let landlords. He now has to travel into town from some distance away, incurring travel as well as similar housing costs.

My current thoughts

THE AREA OF CORE BELIEF	WHAT ARE MY BELIEFS ABOUT BEING PRO-ACTIVE?	WHAT ARE MY BELIEFS ABOUT LEAVING IT TO THE EXPERTS?
Do I have an active or passive attitude to my financial well being?		

What do you actually do right now?

THE AREA OF CORE BELIEF	EXAMPLES OF HOW I AM BEING FINANCIALLY PRO-ACTIVE RIGHT NOW	EXAMPLES OF HOW I AM BEING FINANCIALLY REACTIVE RIGHT NOW
This is how I choose to think about my financial well-being (my economic life)		

Overall, which am I? What evidence exists in my life for that view?

Some more examples of plan-ahead versus wait-and-see.

THOSE WITH ASSETS	THOSE WITHOUT ASSETS
Some people do "what if" thinking about their own finances, to consider the effect of different actions on household cash flow. For example, moving money from a low-performance ISA to one with higher returns	Other people do little "what if" thinking, relying on the action of the employment and property market to provide life's answers

A richer example

The richer Smith family have a goal of mortgage-free living in five years, so reduce their debt at every stage, forgoing a new car or expensive holiday until their goal is reached.

A poorer example

The poorer Jones family expect that their mortgage will go full-term, and rely on job promotion to increase income. Any increase in income is celebrated by a consumer spending event, e.g. splashing out on a new kitchen or car.

How do you measure financial success?

THOSE WITH ASSETS	THOSE WITHOUT ASSETS
Some people know that their overall financial success is measured by the amount of capital (or net assets) employed to make profits	Others know that their financial success is measured by the amount of income currently on show or available to cash in (e.g. housing equity, new car or holiday)

A richer example

The richer Smith family expect to make at least 7% on stock market investments, pension funds and property. They ensure all borrowing is at less than 5% and thus keep a 2% buffer.

A poorer example

The poorer Jones family expect to make whatever they make at their jobs, and whatever the market allows on their pension and property. They have borrowing at rates of 10% and over and aim to minimize their overdraft amount.

Was it possible to identify with any of those? Most of us are a mixture of planner versus catcher-upper. The question is: do your current financial thoughts and behaviours support your search for purposeful profits or not? Does your financial thinking expand or erode your career choices?

The question becomes even more potent if you are working a dual strategy – creating additional income as the work you love is low pay. Given that open chats about personal finance are still a taboo, I hope these questions help you assess how well you are doing against the goal of *Make Money, Be Happy*.

FILL IN THE GAPS.
WHICH PATH ARE YOU ON AND WHERE IS IT TAKING YOU?

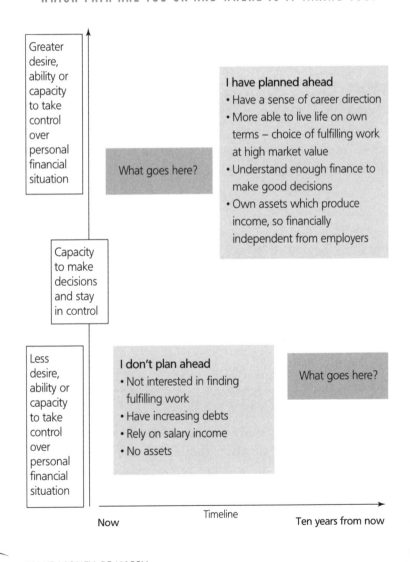

Greater desire, ability or capacity to take control over personal financial situation

Capacity to make decisions and stay in control

Less desire, ability or capacity to take control over personal financial situation

I have planned ahead
• Have a sense of career direction
• More able to live life on own terms – choice of fulfilling work at high market value
• Understand enough finance to make good decisions
• Own assets which produce income, so financially independent from employers

What goes here?

I don't plan ahead
• Not interested in finding fulfilling work
• Have increasing debts
• Rely on salary income
• No assets

What goes here?

Now   Timeline   Ten years from now

Some different attitudes to debt:

THOSE WITH ASSETS	THOSE WITHOUT ASSETS
Some people minimize their gearing (i.e. their borrowings as a percentage of overall capital) to weather inclement economic conditions (e.g. higher interest rates, lower employment). They have a low gearing ratio and a high income gearing ratio	Other people continue to raise their gearing (i.e. their borrowings as a percentage of overall capital) despite weather inclement economic conditions (e.g. higher interest rates, employment). They have a high gearing ratio and a low income gearing ratio

A richer example

The richer Martina reduced her stake in a financial services firm with high bank borrowings in relation to capital. The firm was very profitable, getting large short-term loans from a venture capital house, and selling a large volume of financial products on credit terms. The firm was borrowing to the hilt, turning it into working capital and selling at a profit. However, it was not prepared for difficult economic conditions. So Martina got out, got her money into something safer, and kept the profits.

A poorer example

The poorer Martin increased his small shareholding stake in a football club with high bank borrowings in relation to capital. The club was very profitable, getting large medium-term loans based on TV revenues, and selling a large volume of club merchandise products to wholesalers on credit terms. The football club was borrowing to the hilt, turning it into working capital and selling merchandise at a profit. However, it was not prepared for a difficult season, leading to relegation, reduced ticket and merchandise sales. Martin's money stayed still rather than moving into something safer. He kept the scarf, and the losses.

> **There were times my pants were so thin I could sit on a dime and tell if it was heads or tails.**
> Spencer Tracey, 1900–1967

Many financially independent individuals make financial progress based on the outcomes of their assets, and therefore escape the vagaries of the employment market entirely.

This creates something of a divided society. For example, Roman Abramovitch, the UK's richest person by far in 2004, had at that time a personal net worth of £7.5 billion. His assets work to provide income at a rate of £50k per hour. That's every hour, not just when Chelski are playing. His decisions about where to re-invest that asset-based income are not taken lightly.

Using Mr Abramovitch as a case study we could ask:

- What were his beliefs about how to fund his life (specifically through assets or income)?
- What were his beliefs about the role of advisers in key decisions in his life? Specifically did he take major decisions based on the best available advice (even if expensive) or did he take decisions based on personal experience, limited research and his best personal guess)?
- Did he choose an active role in the big economic decisions impacting his life, or a passive role? For example, did he forecast

what would happen to his career, the industry or professional context it is in, interest rates or other aspects of the economy, and then take action? Or did he play it by ear believing that those things were largely out of his control?

And now back to you:

QUIZ

Are you financially active, or passive?

QUESTION	TRUE	FALSE
1. I think short-term not long-term – the monthly cheque, rather than thinking where this year is going. Forget any further than that.		
2. I tend to spend first, then see what money can be saved, or debt crisis has to be managed afterwards.		
3. I don't understand how money works. For example, I don't understand the difference between income versus assets.		
4. I never check my bank statements. Life is simply too short.		
5. I am not sure if I want to make money, I certainly have not made a decision to be prosperous.		

QUESTION	TRUE	FALSE
6. I believe that my ability, plus hard work will inevitably lead to a prosperous lifestyle. For example, the boss will promote me on merit.		
7. I don't have any financial role models, no wealthy people to observe, and my network consists of people who are not wealthy.		
8. I am not sure what would motivate me to go out and work particularly hard or to create something. I don't really have any sense of a cause, or desire to contribute.		
9. Money is "filthy lucre". Poor people are cooler. Most rich people are sharks with human faces.		
10. Even if I really wanted to, I am not sure I know how to make some serious money.		
11. Right now I just don't feel well enough to make money, my health is holding me back and so I can't do anything to make more money.		

QUESTION	TRUE	FALSE
12. I feel financially constrained by my family. I have dependents that I have to care for, or an extended family that needs me to look after them and therefore I can't risk trying to make more money.		
13. I have got the sense that I am not the sort of person who has money, it wouldn't be me, it wouldn't feel right.		
Totals so far		

Fewer than 7 ticks in the "True" column points to a behavioural pattern of pro-active financial management – but with some weak spots.

More than 7 ticks in the "True" column points to a behavioural pattern of short-termism, and high potential for debt.

These questions are intended to help you become more aware of what could be financial auto-pilot. So you can choose to change, if you want.

How, in the "lack-of-10-minutes-to-read-the-paper" life you already lead, are you going to find time to be your own finance coach? How realistic is it? Well, the evidence is that there are no easy or quick fixes. Darn. It needs some conscious planning and action. Double darn. The good news is, changing your economic destiny could start with missing an hour of rubbish TV each night, to prepare for a career you'll enjoy.

Like, for example, Jim's story.

Jim's story

I worked nights in a bank for 24 years, on their computer systems. Since the takeover they've closed two of the London sites and moved everything and everyone up north. So I'm being made redundant next August. I couldn't work for a boss anymore – that's why I did the Knowledge (Hackney Cab licence training). During the day, when the others were asleep or watching telly I went out learning the streets on my moped and slowly got the exam. It was hard work, but now I've got the taxi I can work hard and always make a bit of money. And I'm glad I did. I was the shift leader and all that, but I hated following orders, especially when they didn't make sense. Like trying to send us all on a motivation course the week after they announced redundancy. I said best leave it. But they'd paid for it already so we had to go. Total waste of time.

The last straw at the bank was last week; I handed in the last performance feedback on the team. My manager said, now Jim you know you can't do this. Do what? I said. You know you have to have a certain percentage in the top ten, say two of the team, the rest in the middle and another two at the bottom. You can't hand in a performance chart with everyone in the top part. But they've all done a brilliant job, I said. Yes, but that's not the way it works Jim. So I had to change it because they had a system that said 10 people in a team can't all go on the top 10% performance, regardless of what actually went on.

Anyway, my mates at the bank are saying I'm lucky to have another job to go to, but I said you could have done the same, but you watched the telly instead. Now some of them are really panicking. You make your own luck. And imagine giving control of your life to the people who come up with a system for rating people like that one.

How do you normally cope if your working life is going through a rough patch? Or if your work doesn't provide for your needs? Do you believe that you can improve the situation and restore a fairly happy workplace equation, or that it is down to others to sort it out?

Happiness is a normal behaviour

Again, your definition is what counts here. We often coast along, assuming that happiness is a natural by-product of being alive. I tend to agree with that, but as life tends to flow in the direction of our dominant thoughts, perhaps it is a good idea to get clear on a personal definition of happiness – so more of it can be created here and now. What does it mean for you? For example, does happiness mean:

- More time with people you love (NB always check this is reciprocated . . .).
- More fulfilment from your work.
- More quiet time.
- Feeling healthy and well.
- More loud time – music and clubs and every tune your gizmo can hold.
- More sex and stuff and rock and roll.
- Greater sense of security and confidence about the future.
- Living life to the full – exercise, travel and adventure.
- Feeling loved and able to share your love (no singing please).
- Time to travel and explore.
- What else for you – add here . . .

Happiness might also include more connection to others:

- Better sense of community.
- Loving family relationships.

- Optimism about improving the environment, or local area.
- Desire to look after our home properly (that includes the environment).
- Feeling of belonging.
- Collective desire for public, as well as private, good.

What does your definition of a perfectly happy day consist of? Or a perfectly happy afternoon at work (or is that a contradiction in terms?) A perfectly happy evening?

If you don't know, try to find out. How tough can it be?

Action

> Our deeds determine us, as much as we determine our deeds. George Eliot, 1859

Now, down to the part where you apply your own ideas, to *Make Money, Be Happy*. It does depend on where you are. So once again – take a look.

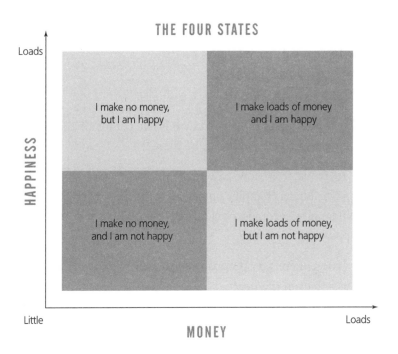

THE FOUR STATES

Loads

HAPPINESS

I make no money,
but I am happy

I make loads of money
and I am happy

I make no money,
and I am not happy

I make loads of money,
but I am not happy

Little

Loads

MONEY

Make purposeful profit

(If you found yourself in the top-right corner on the grid, or want to be there.)

Would you like to make the right amount of money, doing the thing you most want to do? Work that feels most meaningful, purposeful, fulfilling to you. This is an integrated strategy for both money and fulfilment.

Fund your fulfilment – the Dual Strategy

(If you found yourself in the top-left corner of the grid, or want to be there.)

When what you love to do doesn't pay the bills. This is where you will learn how to create a separate income strategy to ensure you retain the ability to do work that most fulfils you. You don't give up on your dreams because of the need to pay the mortgage.

Anywhere's better than this . . .

(If you found yourself in the bottom-left corner of the grid – does anyone actively choose to be there?)

How to move from low pay, low fulfilment work to a better place. The bigger, happier choice is to be anywhere but here. Anywhere else becomes a big other. This is about the first steps to happiness and money.

Your actions here are: purpose check, debt loss, value add and then assets from the heart.

Resign from lying

(If you found yourself in the bottom-right corner of the grid, or want to be there.)

How to detach gently from a job which undermines the true you, so you can uncover what you really want. Do you want to resign from a life of compromise, and start to build opportunities based on your real priorities? This chapter considers how to make money, but this time without loss of your soul. This is also an excellent staging post if you've moved from the bottom-left corner of the grid.

Your actions here are the purpose check, and if you find yourself stuck in salary-based income only, consider how to get some assets from the heart sooner rather than later.

The Make Money, Be Happy strategy – in practice

Perhaps this is a good moment to follow one example through in detail.

Melanie is an architect aged 27. She earns £25k and rents a flat with two others. Her magic number (the amount of monthly disposable income after debts and all costs) is around £140 per month. She is doing well professionally and loves her job, but has lots of student debt and is probably going to see only small increases in her salary for the next two or three years.

Current asset strategy – pay a small amount each month into a private pension. That's all.

Melanie is in the top-left corner of the four states grid – moving towards the right. She makes some money and is happy at work. This is a great situation – the question is how to improve her market value (and therefore income) by adding more value at work. Then use disposable income to pay off debts with a parallel strategy to gently build assets from the heart.

The value add strategy

■ Melanie could do more to understand how her firm works – learn about the end-to-end process of value add (yes, it sounds boring). She loves her work, but has not learned relationship skills or how to put herself in the shoes of a client to see the firm and/or her role, through their eyes.

■ Melanie needs to understand how her architectural skills are costed into a project to make money for the firm. She leaves the money side to someone else.

■ Melanie could also learn about where the company or organization is heading and what its future plans are, i.e. become interested in the decisions of the company and become one of the band of future planners.

- Or understand enough about the management and money as well as the professional specialism to be able to consider branching out into a new practice one day.

- Sometimes greater learning comes from extra responsibility, and so, without going over the top, Melanie could take on tasks with higher levels of difficulty, and requiring extra skills. She could gain an even more specialist skill – such as computer-aided design or bid management, which are of high value to the organization.

The debt loss plan

- Melanie has high amounts of debt and instead of dealing with it, finds it easier to just scrape through each month.

- She could create a one-month spending log to work out where the money goes.

- Prioritize highest interest debts first.

- Use the spending log to find some money that would be better spent reducing debt. (For example, those vast lattes each day).

- Talk to the lenders and agree a repayment schedule on any extreme cases (shouldn't need to here).

- Decide "I'm not creating debt – just today" to put a brake on impulse or emotional spending. Work out the triggers for over-spending – is there a particular mood, location or situation that brings out the credit card everytime? Noticing them is halfway to ending them. Melanie has store card debts from her (normal) desire to appear fabulous for special occasions – and lots of her friends have got married in the past year!

Assets of the heart strategy

- Make sure debts are paid off first. No point in investing for a 10% return while paying off a store card at 24%.

- Decide how much of the disposable income can be spent. Surely you want to have some "just spend it on who cares what" cash?

- Once that is decided, investigate assets with most personal connection. What investments appeal and would be a buy from the heart?
- For example – could Melanie invest in the firm she works for? Does that option exist?
- Or property development opportunities available to architects – do preferential schemes exist?
- Or investing in Ethical Property developments – offering long-term shares to investors seeking to invest in property used for social enterprise.
- Or property close to where she grew up in Scotland.
- Melanie then needs to work out the likely returns in those areas and do some research into buying shares – with or without an adviser.
- Then buy small amounts each month. For example, some long-term shares in her own firm, some in a high yield property bond and the rest saved for a deposit to buy a collectively owned property with five friends. Very sensible.

And just a reminder of some of the practical strategies that Melanie could adopt to add more value and income.

1 **The hard work option** – add hours, add energy, or work for a wider audience.
2 **The premium option** – become known as the best, aim for shorter hours for same or greater reward.
3 **The media option** – become a pundit, someone whose opinion is valued by the media.
4 **The consulting option** – take the role of advocate for the customer or client for example.
5 **The contribution option** – find a way to give more of what you love.
6 **The contract-out option** – find a way to broker a win–win.

Clearly these strategies take time to come to fruition. In a world of instant gratification, choosing to focus on the most fulfilling aspects of your job, and creating a sound commercial path alongside that isn't going to happen in 20 minutes. Going back to the concept of natural laws, seeds need some time to grow before harvest. Though many of us seem intent on changing everything just because it doesn't feel instantly right. A bit like digging up damp, recently planted seeds on a regular basis!

I hope by now that you will be feeling strategy rich. The question is, are you going to be able to put those strategies to good use in your own life? Concluding this section on action, I have pulled together a number of *"Make Money, Be Happy"* themes into a relatively straightforward process.

Six steps anyone can take to Make Money, Be Happy

6 Do what you want to do. *Make Money, Be Happy*

- For instance, do you want to leave your current job to retrain in a more creative role? Work out how much your assets will need to provide to be able to do that?
- Same with travel, or social change work.
- Do your cash projections and figure out how much fulfilment your assets can fund. Fully funded – what are you waiting for?
- Or do you love your current job, and prefer to gain most of your income through salary. Great. You are also more secure, able to take risks at work with the confidence from your other income streams.

5 Buy assets – from the heart

- When debts are sorted, select which of the many assets will bring you most happiness, and make the most money.
- Spend an affordable amount of surplus income on those preferred assets.
- Keep learning more about them, understand their yield, performance and potential risks.
- Enjoy building a portfolio of assets you are interested in – and watch income grow from them.

4 Pay off debts with surplus income

Congratulations. Your improved value add + negotiation has resulted in more income. Now use that income to:

- First, pay off high interest debts.
- Second, begin to research your preferred assets to invest in.
- Remember to be good to yourself in the meantime.

1 Learn the value of your work to your employer

- For instance, how do you use your skills, experience and all-round talent to make the customer happy?
- Understand how and why your value add becomes your current salary. Increase your knowledge of the overall job market and on the competitiveness of salaries with similar positions in your field.

2 Add more value (and thus become more valuable)

- Understand how your organization works – learn about the end-to-end process of value add. Put yourself in the shoes of a user or customer and see your role through their eyes. What do you do that makes money or creates a valued service?
- Learn about where the company or organization is heading and what its future plans are.
- Sometimes greater learning comes from extra responsibility, and so, without going over the top, take on tasks with higher levels of difficulty, and requiring extra skills. Gain specialist skill which is of high value to the organization.

3 Negotiate and earn more

- Use your knowledge to solve higher value problems. Advise at a more senior level or to more people. Become a trusted advisor as much as a trusted do-er. Become the customer advocate in-house. Know the profit you create.
- Make sure your value add is widely understood.
- Use your market knowledge to negotiate with your employer to earn the best possible rate.

1 Learn the value of your work to your employer

■ For instance, how do you use your skills, experience and all-round talent to make the customer happy?

■ Understand how and why your value add becomes your current salary.

■ Increase your knowledge of the overall job market and on the competitiveness of salaries with similar positions in your field.

■ Plus – add your ideas here . . .

■

■

2 Add more value (and thus become more valuable)

■ Understand how your organization works – learn about the end-to-end process of value add. Put yourself in the shoes of a user or customer and see your role through their eyes. What do you do that makes money or creates a valued service?

■ Learn about where the company or organization is heading and what its future plans are.

■ Sometimes greater learning comes from extra responsibility, and so, without going over the top, take on tasks with higher levels of difficulty, and requiring extra skills. Gain specialist skill which is of high value to the organization.

■ Plus – add your ideas here . . .

■

■

3 Negotiate and earn more

■ Use your knowledge to solve higher value problems. Advise at a more senior level or to more people. Become a trusted adviser as much as a trusted do-er. Become the in-house customer advocate. Know the profit you create.

- Make sure your value add is widely understood.
- Use your market knowledge to negotiate with your employer to earn the best possible rate.
- Plus – add your ideas here . . .
-
-

4 Pay off debts with surplus income

Congratulations. Your improved value add + negotiation has resulted in more income. Now use that income to:

- First, pay off high interest debts.
- Second, begin to research your preferred assets to invest in.
- And remember to be good to yourself in the meantime.
- Plus – add your ideas here . . .
-
-

5 Buy assets – from the heart

- When debts are sorted, select which of the many assets will bring you most happiness, and make the most money.
- Spend an affordable amount of surplus income on those preferred assets.
- Keep learning more about them, understand their yield, performance and potential risks.
- Enjoy building a portfolio of assets you are interested in – and watch income grow from them.
- Plus – add your ideas here . . .
-
-

6 Do what you want to do. Make Money, Be Happy

- For instance, do you want to leave your current job to retrain for a more creative role? Work out how much your assets will need to provide to be able to do that?
- Same with family time, travel, or social change work.
- Do your cash projections and figure out how much fulfilment your assets can fund. Fully funded – what are you waiting for?
- Or do you love your current job, and prefer to gain most of your income through salary? Great. You are also more secure, able to take risks at work with the confidence from your other income streams.
- Plus – add your ideas here . . .
-
-

Action – the facts about my value add

It might be an idea to note down how much you now know about your value, and your capacity to make more money and be even happier.

1 This is how much my working time is worth, per day, to my current employer. This is because . . .

2 This is how much I feel it is worth (if different from item 1 above) . . .

3 My calculation of that figure is as follows: . . .

4 List those who would:

(a) agree . . .

(b) disagree . . .

5 Would that rate change if my work felt hugely creative, worthwhile and fulfilling? If yes, why?

6 Do I naturally live within my available income level, or rely on credit cards and other borrowings?

7 If I had surplus money from work, how would I choose to spend it? Have I identified any assets close to my heart . . .

8 How do I spend my free time outside of work? How many hours does that mean? And then calculate each percentage of the following:

- Family time ....%
- Spending money ....%
- Sleeping ....%
- Creative time ....%
- Exercise ....%
- Socializing ....%
- Resting ....%
- Eating (and food-related efforts) ....%
- Cleaning ....%
- Other activity 1 ....%
- Other activity 2 ....%
- Other activity 3 ....%

9 How would a huge lump sum of money (say one million pounds) change my view of work? . . .

10 How would I feel about asking my boss to pay a day rate for my work, e.g. contracting or consulting instead of being an employee? Would I have a personal pricing strategy? . . .

11 Do I know the costs to the firm of having me as an employee? . . .

12 What do I know about the salary for my job in comparable companies?
   (a) Who could you ask for more information on this? . . .
   (b) What other resources are available? . . .

13 What do I know about consultancy or contract rates for my current job?
   (a) Who could you ask for more information on this? . . .
   (b) What other resources are available? . . .

14 What are my current financial goals? List under the following categories:
   (a) Target income (please state exact amount) . . .
       Timescale (by – please give exact date) . . .

   (b) The reason why you will be paid that income – from the point of view of customers or employers . . .

(c) Target debt (er – this is about a reduction target!) ...
Timescale (give exact date) ...

(d) Target value of assets ...
Timescale ...

(e) Target income from assets ...
Timescale ...

15 What are my current happiness goals? List under the following categories:
(a) Target career path (give details) ...
(b) Target timescale ...

16 The reason why this and all other responses will really make me happy – from the point of view of family and friends ...
(a) Target homelife ...
Timescale (give exact date) ...

(b) Target health and well-being ...
Timescale ...

(c) Target travel and learning ...
Timescale ...

This is an exercise you might want to do with someone. It may be that the data gathering takes a little time. But you are worth it!

Purposeful profit plus – a formula to Make Money, Be Happy

I have developed a formula that will take you from wherever you are now in your life to someplace better, one which doesn't (necessarily) involve absinthe or a trip to the coast. The formula is a step-by-step method to define your purpose, then align that with a marketplace that wants to pay you money to live it.

A formula to make money and be happy – the employee version

Step 1

My purpose (parts of my job which makes me happy, animates and excites me)

+

my personal package; that which I contribute to my employer so that the organization makes money or provides a useful service (this includes my experience, personal and professional network, expertise, financial status and character assets – both tangible and intangible. Another description would be my measurable value add)

=

my purposeful products or services.

Step 2

My purposeful product or service

+

external demand in the form of a job which provides salary and bonus

=

my market value.

Step 3

My market value

×

amount of time being bought by the employer

=

my total income or my purposeful profits or gross revenue.

Step 4

Purposeful profits

−

lifestyle costs

=

Make Money, Be Happy. **A way to live your life so that it contains more of what is most important to you.**

A formula to make money and be happy – the consultancy or freelance version

Step 1

My purpose (that which makes me happy, which animates and excites me)

+

my personal package (my experience, personal and professional network, expertise, financial status and character assets – both tangible and intangible)

=

my purposeful products or services.

Step 2

My purposeful product or service

+

external demand (buyers, employers, customers)

=

my market value.

Step 3

My market value

×

sales volume

=

my purposeful profits or gross revenue.

Step 4

Purposeful profits

−

lifestyle costs

=

Make Money, Be Happy. **A way to live your life so that it contains more of what is most important to you.**

Now that condenses a lot into a few lines. Next comes the detail.

Step-by-step formula

Step 1 – My purposeful products or services

Q What do I need to know, to be able to do the Step 1 calculation?

A The answer comes from answering the following checklist of questions.

How to find purpose. A nice easy checklist!

Your purpose in life is to be happy. To find and fund your own fulfilment. How you live your own version of happiness is up to you – that is the delicious detail of designing a successful life. You are architect, playwright, personal trainer, travel guide uniquely qualified to create the most loving, enjoyable success story imaginable. The source of your success is locating your own, unique kind of happiness.

If you find these questions are hard to answer, consider doing a self-interview. Or imagine that your best friend is answering these questions based on what they know about you.

Just list down as many answers as come to mind. You may want to use material from my book *Soultrader* or from earlier chapters here.

A purpose checklist

1 What makes me happy – when do I feel most relaxed and contented? What am I doing, who am I with?

2 What is my favourite daydream about my success?

3 If I were to be a superheroine (or hero) for a day, which one would I be? Why? (NB Scooby Doo is not a superhero. Nor is Lemony Snicket. Oh all right then.)

4 What aspects of my personality or character am I most proud of?

5 What has been my proudest moment, ever?

6 Who loves me?

7 When was the last time I decided to make something happen – with perfect success? (NB This could be the last time you decided to find mango ice cream, or to change your career!)

8 In what ways might I self-sabotage my own happiness?

9 What would my most perfect afternoon contain, as outrageous treats for my senses?

10 Who do I love?

11 What scares me most right now about how my life is working?

12 What is the opposite of that last question?

13 How would my friends describe my life so far?

14 How many happy moments come to mind in the past week?

Am I eligible for purposeful profits?

1 What aspect of my job makes me most happy?

2 What has been the most wonderful moment of peer appreciation in my career so far? For what?

3 What drives me to do what I do right now – what are the main reasons why I go to work?

4 If I found a magic wand in my bag one morning, what would my three workplace wishes be?

5 What is the most common irritation in my working life right now?

6 What would my boss write on a page entitled "the next two years for this team"

7 What would I write?

8   What dreams do I have – what do I most want to achieve?

9   In a work context, what do I offer that makes others happy – be they colleagues or customers or clients? How do I know?

10 What am I really good at, using my skills, expertise and experience?

11 Being honest, what do I seriously need to improve on?

12 Who would I most like to be mentored by and why?

13 What is my current net income and current set of costs per month?

14 Overall, do I make a monthly profit or loss on my current work choice?

15 What would I like to earn in one year's time?

16 What assets do I have?

See Section 4 for content and exercises to help you define your purpose and personal package, as well as any brakes and accelerators in this area.

Outcomes from Step 1

■ Define your life purpose.

■ Define and document the strengths and weaknesses of your personal package.

■ Work out the brakes and accelerators for this stage.

■ Know where you are at the moment.

■ Work out a timescale for the first action.

Step 2 – My market value

Q What do I need to know, to be able to do the Step 2 calculation?

A The answer comes from answering the following checklist of questions.

A checklist of questions to discover my market value

■ What demand exists, i.e. who would buy my purposeful product or service?

■ Do I understand the factors driving demand for my services?

■ Is my salary the right market price for what I do?

■ What is the economic value of my labour?

■ Do I let my employer know their return on investment for my labour?

■ The number of buyers drives my price – so, how can I stimulate their interest?

■ Why should they buy from me – do I have any unique selling points (USPs)?

■ What is the competition?

■ What other factors drive the market value right now (local or time-sensitive factors)?

See Section 3 for content and exercises to help you (a) work out demand; (b) work on your USP (stated in the language of the market); (c) work on brakes and accelerators (e.g. a habit of underearning, low confidence); (d) get clearer on why you want to do this.

Outcomes from Step 2

▨ Definition of demand for your purposeful product or service.

▨ Definition of market value.

▨ Work out the brakes and accelerators for this stage.

▨ Know where you are at the moment.

▨ Work out next steps (sort out gaps, take baby steps).

Step 3 – My purposeful profits or gross revenue

Q What do I need to know, to be able to do the Step 3 calculation?

A The answer comes from answering the following checklist questions.

A checklist of questions to understand my purposeful profits

▨ How much of your purposeful product will your customers want to buy?

▨ How could you maximize distribution of your purposeful product or service?

▨ Could this be as a franchise, or through existing agents?

▨ How to turn these profits into assets which do not require any daily attention?

See pages 207–211 for content and exercises to help you (a) define sales; (b) define likely sales volume; (c) define profits; (d) how to turn profits into assets.

Outcomes from Step 3

▨ Definition of sales volume for your purposeful product or service.

▨ Definition of purposeful profits.

▨ Work out the brakes and accelerators for this stage.

- Know where you are at the moment.
- Work out next steps (sort out gaps, take baby steps).

Step 4 – Make Money, Be Happy

Q What do I need to know, to be able to do the Step 4 calculation?

A The answer comes from answering the following checklist of questions.

A checklist of questions to Make Money, Be Happy
- Do you understand your current financial status?
- Can you define the daily costs of living your true purpose?
- Do you understand how to reduce your debt levels?

See pages 82–85 for content and exercises to help you (a) define debts and other day-to-day lifestyle costs; (b) calculate earnings from purposeful products (*"Make Money, Be Happy"*)

Outcomes from Step 4
- Definition of your current financial situation.
- Definition of how much your life costs, and what profit you currently make.
- Work out the brakes and accelerators for this stage.
- Know where you are at the moment.
- Work out next steps (sort out gaps, take baby steps).

Step 5 – Make Money, Be Happy – forever

Q What do I need to know, to be able to do the Step 5 calculation?

A Become aware of where you are at any one time, and where you want to go next, living your purpose and making money.

See page 97 for content and exercises to help you (a) see the lifecycle of *Make Money, Be Happy*; (b) be clear on daily habits in terms of beliefs, behaviour and actions; (c) enjoy where you are now.

Outcomes from Step 5

- Definition of how to work out your next purposeful product or service.
- Definition of what must be in place at each stage.
- Work out the brakes and accelerators for this stage.
- Know where you are at the moment.
- Work out next steps (sort out gaps, take baby steps).

Finally, an introduction

This book has been really challenging to write! I have distilled learning from my own experience, alongside ideas from a wide range of professional disciplines ranging from economics, business and psychology. But more than that, I have tried to write something which has practical application, whatever the individual reader situation. It has been challenging because the lessons are from real life, but I didn't want lots of case study stories. The focus has to be on you, your transition, your priorities.

I hope the exercises help get you back on intimate terms with your own values, so that you can build prosperity while keeping your soul intact. The free market system is here to stay, and you and I can choose to use it for our personal advancement. Or we can keep working, spending and owing, with no great sense of control. *Make Money, Be Happy* has been written to equip you in that competitive marketplace. I bang on about linking your happiness to the customer happiness because, from Ford to Hewlett Packard to Apple, endless business case studies show that when a company gets passionate about what makes customers happy, performance improves, creativity goes into better products and services, and the profits start rolling in. The firm gets to make money and be happy. Exactly the same lessons apply to you as an individual employee. How can you maximize what makes you happy at work in a way that maximizes what makes your customer happy? So if you don't know how your workplace creates happy customers (or users in a not-for-profit environment) I suggest that is the first priority.

Perhaps you'll want to spend the next 20 years making customers happy. Great. You'll have found your purposeful profit. But if, as the trends show, you will want to intersperse times of full employment with time off with your family, your mind, your travelling free spirit, you'll need to have a way to fund your fulfilment, outside the normal rules of work. The dual strategy.

Finally, the book recognizes that economic inequality is a fact of life. Assets beget assets just as poverty begets poverty, so one goal is, simply, get your life back into solvency. That's what I need to do. It was like a voice saying "if you want justice in the world, start by sorting out your own problems". So after ten years working out my own dual strategy, I was financially independent and able to step out of full-time employment and get back on the social justice path. It did take ten years though. For you, it could take a lot less. I hope so.

I cannot offer you any bigger encouragement than the words in this book and I do offer them with all my heart.

Thank you for reading. If you'd like more resources, take a look at www.makemoneybehappy.com or carmel@makemoneybehappy.com for email.

Now, please, go *Make Money, Be Happy* yourself.

And let me know how it goes?

Further reading

Make money

Built to Last, James C. Collins and Jerry I. Porras (Random House, 2004)

The New Rules, John P. Kotter (The Free Press, 1995)

The Affluent Society, John Kenneth Galbraith (Penguin Books, 1999)

Capital, Karl Marx (Penguin Books, 2002)

Think and Grow Rich, Napoleon Hill (Vermilion, 2004)

Rich Dad Poor Dad, Robert T. Kiyosaki (Little Brown, 2000)

Free Lunch, David Smith (Profile Books, 2003)

Know Your Value?, Mick Cope (FT Prentice Hall, 2000)

The Strategy and Tactics of Pricing, Thomas T. Nagle and Reed K. Holden (Prentice Hall, 2001)

The Wealth of Nations, Adam Smith (Bantam Classics, 2003)

Creating Money, Sanaya Roman and Duane Packer (HJ Kramer, 1988)

Business as Unusual, Anita Roddick (PerfectBound, 2001)

Debt Free by 30, Jason Anthony and Karl Cluck (Plume Books, 2001)

Ben and Jerry's Double Dip, Ben Cohen and Jerry Greenfield (Simon & Schuster, 1999)

World Class Customer Satisfaction, Jonathan D. Barsky (McGraw-Hill, 1996)

Be happy

The Work We Were Born to Do, Nick Williams (Element Books, 2000)

Creating a Life Worth Living, Carol Lloyd (HarperCollins, 1997)

The Art of Happiness, His Holiness the Dalai Lama (Hodder & Stoughton, 1999)

The Progress Paradox: How Life Gets Better While People Feel Worse, Gregg Easterbrook (Random House, 2003)

Staying Sane, Raj Persaud (Bantam, 2001)

What is Good, A.C. Grayling (Phoenix, 2004)

Career Anchors, Edgar H. Schein (Pfeiffer Wiley, 1985)

Willing Slaves, Madeleine Bunting (HarperCollins, 2004)

Being Happy, Andrew Matthews (Media Masters, 1989)

Feel the Fear and Do It Anyway, Dr Susan Jeffers (Rider, 1997)

In Praise of Slow, Carl Honore (Orion, 2004)

Finding Flow: The Psychology of Engagement with Everyday Life, Mihaly Csikszentmihalyi (MasterMinds, 1998)

The Happiness Equation, Manfret Ket de Vries (Vermilion, 2002)

And a few I made earlier

Float You – How to Capitalize on your Talent, co-authored with Mick Cope (momentum, 2001)

Careers Un-ltd – How to Choose a Career That Deserves You, co-authored with Jonathan Robinson (momentum, 2002)

Soultrader – Find Purpose, and You'll Find Success, just me (momentum, 2002)

Resources – debt

Citizens Advice Bureau (CAB)   Offers free advice about credit and money issues from 700 local bureaux. Search for your nearest CAB online.
Website: www.nacab.org.uk

Consumer Credit Counselling Service (CCCS)   A free confidential advice service for people in debt. They can help you to prioritize debts and liaise with creditors on your behalf.
Phone: 0800 138 1111
Website: www.cccs.co.uk
Address: Wade House, Merrion Centre, Leeds, LS2 8NG

Credit Action   National Christian charity, which aims to help people educate themselves about money.
Phone: 01522 699777
Website: www.creditaction.org.uk
Email: office@creditaction.org.uk
Address: The Point, Howard House, Weaver Road, Lincoln LN6 3QN

FCL Debt Clinic   FCL is a free, confidential helpline offering advice and solutions, including supervised arrangements with creditors.
Phone: 0800 716239 (freephone helpline, open 9am–9pm, Mon–Fri)
Website: www.fcl.org.uk
Email: help@debtclinic.co.uk

National Debtline   Phone service offering advice and self-help information packs to those in debt.
Phone: 0808 808 4000 (free and confidential)
Website: www.nationaldebtline.co.uk

The UK Insolvency Helpline   An online resource with a freephone helpline which gives advice to people in debt. The website has a section devoted to student debt – and how to avoid it!
Phone: 0800 074 6918 (freephone helpline, open 24 hours – all year round)
Website: www.insolvencyhelpline.co.uk
Email: info@insolvencyhelpline.co.uk

More resources at www.makemoneybehappy.com